PSYCHOBABBLE & BIOBUNK

USING PSYCHOLOGY TO THINK CRITICALLY
ABOUT ISSUES IN THE NEWS

Opinion essays and book reviews
By Carol Tavris

Library of Congress Cataloging-in-Publication Data

Psychology & biobunk : using psychology to think critically
about issues in the news : opinion essays and book reviews / by
Carol Tavris.—2nd ed.
    p.   cm.
   ISBN 0-13-027986-2
    1. Psychology.   2. Social psychology.   3. Psychotherapy.
    I. Title: Psychobabble and biobunk. II. Tavris, Carol.
BF121.P765   2000
  150—dc21   00-037303
                                      CIP

Psychobabble & Biobunk is for use with *Psychology* and *Invitation to Psychology*, by Carole Wade and Carol Tavris, and also with *Psychology in Perspective*, by Carol Tavris and Carole Wade.

The essays and book reviews in this collection appeared in *The Los Angeles Times* and *The New York Times*, except where noted below. Reprinted by permission.

Pp. 20-22 reprinted with permission of *Skeptic Magazine,* November 1998 by Carol Tavris and Avrum Bluming.

Pp. 23-28 reprinted with permission of *The American Journal of Mental Retardation,* September 1998.

Pp. 53-57 reprinted with permission. Copyright 1998 *Scientific American Inc.* All rights reserved.

 Published by Prentice-Hall, Inc.
A Division of Pearson Education.
Upper Saddle River, NJ 07458

Printed in the United States of America

10 9 8 7 6 5 4

ISBN 0-13-027986-2

Prentice-Hall International (UK) Limited, London
Prentice-Hall of Australia Pty. Limited, Sydney
Prentice-Hall Canada Inc., Toronto
Prentice-Hall Hispanoamericana, S.A., Mexico
Prentice-Hall of India Private Limited, New Delhi
Prentice-Hall of Japan, Inc., Tokyo
Pearson Education Asia Pte. Ltd., Singapore
Editora Prentice-Hall do Brasil, Ltda., Rio de Janeiro

Table of Contents

THE POLITICS AND SCIENCE OF GENDER RESEARCH

APPLYING PSYCHOLOGY TO SOCIAL ISSUES

MENTAL DISORDER AND TREATMENT

A Note to the Reader

Are women and men really two different species, or maybe from two different planets, as so many bestsellers would have us believe? Does a murderer's unhappy background diminish his responsibility for a crime, or is his past irrelevant? Can schools directly instill self-esteem in children, and should they try? Are drugs such as Prozac the answer to most people's emotional problems, or is psychiatric medication an overhyped and oversimplified solution for complex problems?

As citizens, we come across psychological issues like these all the time in the news media, on TV and radio talk shows, and on the Internet. To debate them intelligently, people need to know something about psychological research and how to apply their faculties of critical thinking. Psychology alone does not always provide all the information necessary to make an informed decision, nor will critical thinking always lead to a logical answer; on some topics, people will have to agree to disagree, with abundant evidence and good reasoning on both sides. But we think that psychological research and critical thinking can help enormously. As psychological scientists, we are always amazed (if not amused!) by the number of people perfectly willing to take unyielding positions on complicated issues, without caring at all about the evidence. "I just know that the death penalty deters crime," they will say, or "If you forbid young people to touch alcohol until they are 21, they will then be able to drink sensibly." These are empirical questions on which researchers have gathered considerable data, yet many people cling to the old adage, "My mind's made up; don't bother me with the facts."

The opinion essays and book reviews collected here, written by Carol Tavris for *The Los Angeles Times, The New York Times,* and several magazines (and slightly edited for this volume), show how psychology can be brought to bear on all sorts of matters discussed in the popular culture. We hope the articles will provide a springboard for your own evaluation and analysis of these issues. We know, of course, that there are many points of view on the controversial topics that these articles address, especially "hot button" topics such as pornography, gender roles, the death penalty, abortion, sexual orientation, self-esteem, and parental influence. The articles were written as editorials and express one person's opinions; if you disagree, we encourage you to argue back—as long as you base your own opinion on critical thinking and on evidence that you have mustered to back your position. You don't just get to say, "Phooey, this argument is all wet."

Critical thinking, for us, means the ability and willingness to assess claims and make judgments on the basis of well-supported reasons. Feelings aren't enough, personal experience and anecdotes aren't enough, and shouting down the opposition isn't enough. In our introductory psychology textbooks, we iden-

vii

tify eight guidelines for critical and creative thinking, which we hope you will find useful in thinking about the issues raised by the articles in this collection:

> *Ask questions; be willing to wonder.* To think critically you must be willing to think creatively—to be curious about the puzzles of human behavior, to wonder why people act the way they do, and to question received wisdom and examine new explanations of why things are as they are.

Sample essays that involve this guideline are #3, on the misuses of opinion polls, which invites readers to ask questions about the people who are *not* represented in volunteer surveys and about the consequences of all these opinion polls on people's beliefs and voting behavior; #24, a review of *Flow,* a book that invites readers to question the usual notions of what makes people happy; and #26, which asks readers to consider a question not usually asked in discussions of sexual orientation: What are the origins of *hetero*sexuality?

> *Define your terms.* Identify the problem in clear and concrete terms, rather than vague ones like "happiness," "potential," or "self-esteem."

Sample essays that involve this guideline are #10, on defining what it means to be a "good" mother; #14, on gender differences in friendship, which invites readers to consider that the answer to "which sex is 'better' at intimacy and friendship?" depends on how you define intimacy and friendship; and #25, the meanings of self-esteem and how it is defined: as self-confidence, arrogance, vanity, a sense of self-worth, feelings of competence and mastery, or what?

> *Examine the evidence.* Consider the nature of the evidence supporting various approaches to the problem under examination. *Is* there good evidence, one way or another? Is it reliable? Valid? Is the "evidence" merely someone's personal assertion or speculation, or is it based on replicated empirical data?

Sample essays that involve this guideline are #12, a review of *The Myth of the First Three Years*, a book that critically examines the evidence for the belief that the first three years of life are crucial to a child's intellectual success; and #30, a review of *House of Cards*, a book that assesses the evidence for the successes—and failures—of psychotherapy.

> *Analyze assumptions and biases—your own and those of others.* What prejudices, deeply held values, and other biases do you bring to your evaluation of a problem? Are you willing to consider evidence that contradicts your beliefs? Can you identify the assumptions and biases that others bring to their arguments?

Sample essays that ask readers to examine their deepest assumptions and hold them up honestly to the light of evidence include #11, a review of *The Nurture Assumption,* a book that questions the widely held assumption that parents have the most powerful effect on their children's personality and behavior throughout life; #13, which asks readers to question the widespread assumption that the sexes are inherently "opposite"; and #21, which argues that cultural assumptions and biases about illegal drugs have led to inappropriate and ineffective social policies.

> *Avoid emotional reasoning.* The fact that you feel strongly about something doesn't make you right! Remember that everyone holds convictions about how the world operates (or how it should operate), and your opponents are probably as serious about their convictions as you are about yours. Feelings are important, but they should not substitute for careful appraisal of arguments and evidence.

Some essays that explore the social consequences of emotional reasoning and passionate feelings are #18, a review of *Hystories,* a book examining several current "hysterical epidemics" in American society; #19, which argues that the emotions raised by claims of sexual abuse in day-care centers led to many miscarriages of justice; and #20, on the death penalty.

> *Don't oversimplify.* Look beyond the obvious; reject simplistic thinking ("All the evil in the world is due to that group of loathsome people") and either-or thinking ("Either genes determine everything about personality and behavior or they count for virtually nothing"). Be wary of "argument by anecdote," taking a single case as evidence of a larger phenomenon. For example, reading about one chilling case of a man who murders while on parole should not be the basis on which you assess parole programs in general.

Sample essays that illustrate the problems of either-or thinking, or simplistic analyses of complex problems, include #1, on the appeal of astrology; #5, on the importance of resisting the power of a single anecdote or case study as the basis for forming an opinion on social policy, a candidate, or a political belief; #15, on the "gender gap" in elections, showing why the gap widens and narrows over time; and #28, on why medication for mood disorders is neither totally miraculous nor wholly useless—but why the public is not being given the full story.

> *Consider other interpretations.* Before you draw a conclusion from the evidence, think creatively about other possible explanations. When you learn that two events are statistically correlated, for example, be sure to think care-

fully about which one is the cause and which the result—or whether a third factor might be causing both of them.

Sample essays include #6, on the "illusory correlation" between pornography and rape; #8, a review of *Nonconscious Movements*, a book that offers scientific explanations for apparently mystical phenomena such as "facilitated communication," dowsing, and other procedures involving involuntary hand movements; #22, on the rash of murders by adolescent boys; and #29, which offers an alternative to thinking of "PMS" as a mental disorder.

> *Tolerate uncertainty.* This is probably the hardest step in becoming a critical thinker, for it requires that we hold our beliefs "lightly" and be willing to give them up when better evidence comes along. It requires us to live with the realization that we may not have the perfect answer to a problem at the moment, and may never have it. Many people want "the" answers, and they want science to provide them: "Just tell me what to do!" they demand. Pseudoscience promises answers, which is why it is so popular; science gives us probabilities that suggest that one answer is better than another—for now—and warns us that one day we may have to change our minds.

Essays on this topic include #2, on the appeal of pseudoscientific (and hence often wrong) predictions in our unpredictable world; and #16, a review of *The Two Sexes,* a book arguing that many of the reasons for the rigidly sex typed behavior of children, which typically diminishes as they grow up, may always be a mysterious mixture of biological, cultural, and environmental factors.

We realize that these guidelines are not the only ones possible. They do not include all skills of logic and debate, every principle of scientific reasoning, nor all the mental and emotional obstacles to critical thinking. But we have found that they capture the core elements of scientific and independent thinking. We certainly are aware of our own lapses of critical thinking (which we thoughtfully point out to one another from time to time!), which is why we regard them as ideals to guide our work. We hope that these essays will interest you, amuse you, and, most of all, sharpen your own thoughts about the issues they raise.

Carol Tavris
Carole Wade

A Note to the Instructor

There are many ways to use this collection of essays in the classroom—in courses in psychology, of course, but also in sociology, speech, political science, English composition, and other disciplines. Some instructors may assign the articles as supplementary readings. Others may decide to use them to stimulate class discussions, or assign them as topics for written assignments and exercises. Students can be asked to say why they agree or disagree with the arguments expressed in a given essay, to cite evidence to support their argument, or to identify the critical-thinking guidelines that are most salient in it. They may be asked to think of further questions they would want to raise after reading an article.

For psychology instructors using any of our texts—*Psychology, Invitation to Psychology*, or *Psychology in Perspective*—we offer the following list of topics that are related to the essays in this collection. This list is not exhaustive, but it provides a starting point for showing how research reported in the textbook might be applied to thinking about complex social and psychological issues. And we hope the issues might show why the study of psychology and its methods is so timely, relevant, and important.

Carol Tavris
Carole Wade

ESSAY	RELATED TEXT TOPICS
1. The appeal of pseudoscience 2. The popularity of predictions 3. The misuses of opinion polls 4. The misuses of pop-psych surveys 5. Stories vs. statistics 6. Illusory correlations	Introduction to psychology Principles of critical thinking The scientific method Research methods
7. Alternative medicine	Health, stress, and coping Psychological vs. medical treatments
8. Thinking critically about "mystical messages"	Research methods Facilitated communication Critical thinking The "Barnum Effect"
9. The working mother debate 10. How much influence do mothers have? 11. How much influence do parents have? 12. How critical are the first years of life?	Child development Parental child-rearing practices Behavioral-genetic research on personality and abilities Influences on intelligence and achievement
13. Are men and women "opposite sexes"? 14. The interpretation of differences, I 15. The interpretation of differences, II	Gender development Gender issues in adulthood Theories of gender differences and similarities Cultural psychology
16. The paradox of gender	Gender development and gender typing
17. Biological politics and the study of gender	Sex differences in the brain Evolutionary psychology as related to gender differences
18. Emotional epidemics	Mental disorders The mind-body connection in stress and illness Social psychology (social "contagions") The scientist-practitioner gap
19. The day-care sex-abuse scandals	Children's cognitive development Children's testimony Social influence and conformity

20. The death penalty	Violence and the brain Antisocial personality disorder Issues of "diminished responsibility" in sentencing The uses and misuses of punishment (learning)
21. The war on drugs	Drug use and abuse Addiction Cultural psychology
22. Adolescent violence	Adolescent development Social and cultural origins of violence (e.g., "cultures of honor") Gender differences in expression of anger and depression Peer group influence
23. Bystander apathy	Social psychology, especially discussions of bystander apathy, diffusion of responsibility, deindividuation, and the conditions that foster dissent and altruism
24. The sources of happiness ("flow")	Emotion Optimism and pessimism Stress and health Motivation
25. The meanings of self-esteem	Social learning theory Intrinsic vs. extrinsic motivation Child development Humanist psychology
26. Sexual orientation	Sexual orientation Sexual attitudes and behavior Prejudice
27. Medicating the mind 28. The limits of medication	Medication for mood disorders Biological vs. psychological treatments for mood disorders The scientist-practitioner gap Assessment of psychotherapy
29. The politics of diagnosis: "PMS" and the DSM	The menstrual cycle Hormones and moods Dilemmas of diagnosis Controversies about the DSM
30. Thinking critically about psychotherapy	Assessment of psychotherapy The scientist-practitioner gap

PART I

SCIENCE VERSUS
PSEUDOSCIENCE

1

THE APPEAL OF PSEUDOSCIENCE

This article was written shortly after the news media revealed that former First Lady Nancy Reagan routinely consulted an astrologer before approving her husband's White House schedule. As you read the article, ask yourself: What is the harm in putting one's trust in a pseudoscientific system such as astrology? How do pseudoscientific beliefs violate the principles of critical thinking? Why are they more appealing to some people than the findings of psychological science? And what do you think about politicians who make important decisions based on the alleged alignment of the stars?

Astrology Thrives on the Gullibility Gene

The Los Angeles Times

May 5, 1998

The media have greeted the news of the Reagans' interest in astrology either with amusement or seriousness. One local newscast dutifully presented an astrologer to blather on about why President Reagan gives better press conferences during a full moon or when his Aries is in Aquarius, or whatever.

Certainly the Reagans are in good company. Millions of Americans check their daily horoscope on occasion; I do too, because I always enjoy noting how vague they are, or simply wrong. But there seem to be as many people who are seriously studying astrology these days as there are students of psychology. There is even a new profession—astrologer-psychologist—which combines both occupations. Drop the subject at a party, and the most sober-sided banker or lawyer will tell you conspiratorially about "a birth chart that fit me exactly" or "a prediction that came true absolutely."

Of course, people believe in a vast number of religions and philosophies whose premises they take on faith. I would not object to astrology if it were advertised as a matter of faith. But it is promoted as a science, describing a set of natural laws that affect our lives. As such, astrology consists of testable assumptions: that it can predict future events in nature and in private lives, that the constellation of stars at your birth affects your personality, and so on.

Geoffrey Dean, a scientist who wrote a two-part investigation of astrological claims for The *Skeptical Inquirer*, observes that two questions about astrology are often confused: "Does it work?" and "Is it true?" Many systems "work"—they make people feel better, help them make sense of a complicated world, reassure them that they are normal—without being true. A hundred years ago

3

phrenology, a system of interpreting personality from bumps on the head, was more popular than astrology is today; it wasn't true either, but it "worked" as an effort to explain human behavior.

After major newsworthy events, such as earthquakes or assassinations, articles in astrology journals immediately appear, showing a clear correspondence between the event and its astral alignment. Unfortunately, these predictions are never accurate in advance; if they were, none of us would need disaster insurance.

A U.S. Geological survey once invited astrologers, psychics, and amateur geologists to send in their predictions of future earthquakes. For the 240 predictions made by 27 astrologers, the accuracy rate was worse than had they guessed randomly. In another study of 3,011 predictions made in astrology magazines in the 1970s, only 11 percent turned out to be correct, and many of those were the result of shrewd guesses ("East-west tensions will continue"), vagueness ("A tragedy will hit the east this spring"), or inside information ("Starlet A will marry director B"). Famous astrologers made astonishing blunders, predicting re-elections for heads of state who were assassinated, and vice versa.

Efforts to document the second key tenet of astrology, that one's life and character can be assessed from one's birth chart, also have consistently failed. For example, Geoffrey Dean asked 45 professional astrologers to study 240 birth charts and identify which people were the most introvert-ed, extroverted, emotionally stable or unstable. The astrologers considered the challenge fair and spent nearly 20 hours making their judgments. For comparative purposes, another 45 astrologers simply guessed the traits of each person; this took 20 minutes. The astrologers who analyzed birth charts did no better than those who were guessing; the astrologers did not agree with each other in any case, and supposedly crucial factors, such as the accuracy of the birth date or the astrologers' experience, did not improve the results.

One reason for astrology's continuing popularity is that people are just as happy with wrong charts that have nothing to do with them as they are with the "right" ones. In numerous studies in which people have had to decide which of two or more charts (their own and others) fitted them best, they have never done better than chance. They say that charts generated randomly "fit me exactly," that charts made for someone else "fit me exactly," that all-purpose charts given to thousands of individuals "fit me exactly." As P. T. Barnum said, "Always have a little something for everybody." Astrological descriptions do.

Dean calls astrology "psychological chewing gum, satisfying but ultimately without real substance." If astrology is used as entertainment or religion, he concludes, there is no problem with it. The mind is designed to try to make sense out of experience, to create a coherent story, and astrology does that nicely. Scientist Richard Furnald Smith once said:

"Given the extraordinary ability of the human mind to make sense out of things, it is natural occasionally to make sense out of things that have no sense at all."

But if astrology is advertised as the truth, then consumers are being defrauded and possibly harmed. Powerless people are not served by a philosophy that turns their explanations of destiny to the stars. And when powerful people with ultimate responsibility for the laws and institutions of the nation pass that buck to the stars, the rest of us are in big trouble.

2
THE POPULARITY
OF PREDICTIONS

A hallmark of pseudoscience is certainty. Its practitioners will tell you they know "for sure" that something is so or that a prediction will come true. But scientists speak in the language of probability: They will say something is likely or unlikely to occur. This difference may be one reason that pseudoscience is so popular: When people feel frightened or worried, they welcome predictions that reduce their uncertainty. And yet, a key guideline to critical thinking is the ability to live with some uncertainties—some things that we may never know for sure, or some beliefs we may have to change when new evidence comes along. What kinds of events would you like to be able to predict? What kinds of evidence would you look for to determine whether a prediction is scientifically supported or not?

Call Us Unpredictable

The New York Times

January 2, 1998

Not long ago, while momentarily suffering from end-of-century fever, I agreed to give a talk on "sex and gender in the next millennium." Of course the assignment was preposterous, considering how dramatically the rules of sexuality have changed in the twentieth century.

Who, in 1897, could have predicted transsexuals, sex-chat rooms on the Internet, muscled women running marathons, and ponytailed men changing diapers? Who could have predicted the birth-control pill, cloning, in vitro fertilization, the gay rights movement, legions of women entering business and the military, and legions of Christian men marching on Washington, promising to be faithful and also to wash the dishes?

Nowadays it's hard to make predictions for the next year, let alone for the next 1,000. Most turn out flat wrong because we extrapolate the future from the way things are now, unable to imagine the event or discovery that will change the world. At the end of the nineteenth century, for instance, city planners in New York predicted that traffic would soon come to a standstill. There would be far too many horses, and too many tons of horse manure, for anyone to be able to move. Throughout history, many experts who should have known better have likewise succumbed to the temptation to predict:

- In 1895, Lord Kelvin, president of the Royal Society in England, said, "Heavier-than-air flying machines are impossible."
- In 1929, Irving Fisher, professor of economics at Yale, said, "Stocks have reached what looks like a permanently high plateau."
- In 1958, Thomas J. Watson, the chairman of I.B.M., said, "I think there is a world market for about five computers."

Predictably, predictions haven't improved over time. According to the *Skeptical Inquirer's* annual review of New Year's predictions by psychics, 1997 was supposed to be the year that Mick Jagger became a member of Parliament, Congress suspended the baseball season after a brawl left dozens of people dead or wounded, and Hillary Clinton got pregnant again.

Considering these dud forecasts, I sometimes think the only thing anyone can predict with confidence is that human beings will continue making predictions, because we are a naturally anxious and insecure species that wants to know what the future holds.

Today, especially, the world seems to be spinning out of control. How are we supposed to fight the impersonal corporate decisions that affect our daily lives, when we can't even cope with those infernal voice-mail menus? No wonder so many people seek to restore a sense of control over life by reaching for the simplified explanations and forecasts provided by demagogues, gurus, psychics, and pseudoscientists.

Even sophisticated urbanites are not immune. In 1999 an article in *Smithsonian* magazine reported that hundreds of New Yorkers and other "urban New Agers" were using dowsing rods to decide "everything from stock market buys to whether they should respond to an ad in the Personals." If New Yorkers are dowsing for stocks and dates, we can be sure that anxiety about money and love is up (and scientific literacy is down).

Pseudoscientific predictions are more appealing than the sober predictions of science for two reasons. First, pseudoscientists speak in the reassuring tones of certainty: This *will* happen. Scientists speak in the annoying language of probability: It is *likely* that this will happen.

Most scientific predictions apply to groups of trends, not individuals or specific events. Thus, scientists can predict with great accuracy that smoking will increase the likelihood of earlier death, but they cannot predict that any given smoker will get lung cancer. But most individuals want to know what, specifically, will happen to them. Science can't say.

Second, pseudoscientific predictions are appealing because they are based on intuition, faith, compelling anecdote or individual experience. That makes them as unreliable as guessing, although they seem accessible, personal and dramatic. Scientists rely on statistical probabilities derived from objective evidence. That makes their predictions often highly accurate, although they seem tentative, remote, and encumbered with qualifications.

Of course, it's harmless and fun to make silly predictions at the end of every year. But the larger question—on what basis should we make predictions for ourselves and believe those made by others?—is serious, because it affects so many decisions, big and small, that we make about our lives.

Perhaps the major difference between scientists and pseudoscientists is that the former know what they can't predict, whereas the latter will predict anything you ask them to. On that note, care to join me in making any predictions about sex and gender in this new millennium?

3

THE MISUSES OF OPINION POLLS

Most of us regard opinion polls as a simple fact of modern life; we may view them as entertaining, informative, or thought-provoking, but rarely do we consider them dangerous. This essay was written in 1988, long before Bill Clinton and other politicians of the 1990s came to rely on polls not only for campaign decisions during elections, but also for policy decisions while in office. After reading this article, ask yourself what your opinion is of opinion surveys. Would you respond to one yourself? How much credence do you give to the numbers bandied about on talk radio? Which polls (if any) are useful, and which might we be better off without?

For Whom Do The Polls Toll?
The Silenced Majority

The Los Angeles Times

October 14, 1988

As a social scientist who was trained in survey research, I'm angry at the mad proliferation of polls, the scientific ones and the unscientific ones. The country has gone completely round the bend on this. It's as if we can't make a decision about a candidate, a policy, or even a movie unless we feel that we share the majority view. "Safety in numbers," we cry, as the numbers drown us.

Consider the growing popularity of that pseudo-poll, the volunteer call-in vote. In Los Angeles, a talk-show host invited his listeners to call the station and vote on who "won" a vice-presidential debate. "This isn't a sci-entifically accurate poll," he said coyly, but "it does reflect a cross-section of the population." The disclaimer is irrelevant; it implies that the results are meaningful when they are not. A bunch of volunteer callers doesn't represent anyone but themselves, no matter how varied their place on the spectrum. Strange though it may seem to the statistically uninitiated, the responses of a randomly selected sample of 1,000 people can tell you what 140 million people believe; a sample of 10,000 people who have volunteered their opinions tells you only what those 10,000 believe.

Of course, radio and television encourage audience participation because it is entertaining and it helps the ratings. Well, what's wrong with that? Isn't it all just a game? No, it isn't. Special interest groups that hold minority opinions can organize call-ins, trying to create the impression with numbers that theirs is a majority view.

I'm not fond of professional public opinion polls, either. For one thing, that's just what they measure: opinion, as opposed to conviction. That is why survey results about the candidates change so often and are so unreliable, varying according to the respondent's mood and the phrasing of questions. The polls do not discriminate between informed people whose political views are anchored in a broader philosophy, and those who make voting decisions based, as one radio caller plans to do, on one candidate's eyes (she likes them) rather than another's hair (she dislikes it). Further, polls tell us only how people say they will vote; but often what people tell a pollster bears little relation to what they actually do when they are in the voting booth.

The obsession with polls is hazardous to our political and psychological health. Not only are politicians becoming increasingly reliant on them for policy decisions, but polls also are succeeding in bullying and silencing people who are led to believe that they are a minority.

Americans don't like to be out of step. For all our much-vaunted individualism, we feel that it is somehow unAmerican to be different. Psychologists Gary Marks and Norman Miller have identified a common human delusion they call the "false consensus effect": the tendency for people to believe that their own desires, beliefs, and even personal problems are shared by the majority. By overestimating the degree of agreement between themselves and others, people maintain their self-esteem, reduce the discomfort of inconsistency or feeling "weird," and maintain the conviction that they are right.

All that is normal, but it is troubling for democracy. Some people with minority views respond by trying to persuade everyone (and themselves) that they are the majority. Others with minority views respond with apathy and depression: "There's no point doing anything," they say. "There's no point voting for a loser." So they stop speaking up, or voting, thereby creating a self-fulfilling prophecy.

All of this is why, during elections, I'm going to try to ignore the pollsters and make my decision about the candidates based on more than "who's ahead." And, perhaps irrationally, I will hope that on election day the majority of voters will make their decisions on something other than the latest poll—or on the color of a candidate's eyes.

4

THE MISUSES OF POP-PSYCH SURVEYS

Psychology students sometimes complain about having to study methodology, but no topic is more important for anyone hoping to be scientifically (and psychologically) literate. Can you tell the difference between social science and "social science fiction"? Is there some information that an unrepresentative survey such as Hite's might legitimately contribute, despite its shortcomings? What's wrong with drawing statistical conclusions from such work?

Method Is All But Lost in the Imagery of Social Science Fiction

The Los Angeles Times

November 1, 1987

When Shere Hite's book, *Women and Love*, was published, it was accorded the dignity of ground-breaking science: Serious-sounding statistics announced that such-and-such a number of all women are unhappy in their relationships; such-and-such a number of all women feel that men don't listen to them, and so on.

Hite may be right about women, but not because of her numbers. The numbers are, to put it simply, a joke. Hite mailed out 100,000 "questionnaires"—like her other two surveys, this one was biased and unprofessional in its construction of questions—and got a four percent return from a sample of women who were in no way representative of all American women. This return rate is what you would pray for if you were in the junk-mail business or if you were starting a magazine and wanted to ascertain public interest from a direct-mail campaign. If you were a survey researcher hoping for a credible sample, you would be obliged to start over, or perhaps consider another line of work.

Hite is very sensitive about the question of her methods. She devotes a chapter to defending subjective routes to truth, and then tries to convince the reader that her work is objective and scientifically accurate as well. (When the manuscript of the book was sent to magazines around the country for possible excerpting, this chapter was missing; it appeared only in the final, bound book. This means that many news reporters and editors had to make their decisions about the worthiness of the book without knowing how Hite got her results.)

11

Well, what is wrong with subjective routes to truth? Why not publish some articulate complaints by women?

The answer, I think, lies in the growing popularity of what Robert Asahina, a writer and editor, called "social science fiction"—books that are not really social science, but "naive personal journalism." The authors' efforts to maintain that their ideas are based on "research" adds a veneer of respectability and seriousness and supposedly elevates them above the authors' personal experiences.

Of course, many times social scientists conduct research on unrepresentative samples. Many have drawn inappropriate conclusions about all of humanity from studies of white male sophomores. Sex researchers, including Kinsey, have always had to rely on the kindness of strangers who would be willing to answer impertinent questions. I myself confess to having conducted surveys for *Psychology Today* and *Redbook*, in which I was lucky if respondents represented the readership, much less the whole country. (I always acknowledged this in reporting the results.) And all social scientists appreciate the value of subjective routes to truth from personal experience, armchair observations of the world, and dinner conversations with friends.

But there are several critical differences between social science and social science fiction. Scientists understand that a study is only one fragment of the mosaic; this is why they are at pains to cite other research, both confirming and critical, along with their own. They are aware of the many sources of distortion in research: in the experimenter's own expectations, in the biases of volunteers, in the way instructions and questions are worded. They understand that what people say is only tenuously related to what they do. They begin with a hypothesis that they seek to *disprove*.

The writers of social science fiction do just the opposite. They rarely investigate or cite other research; they cheerfully ignore problems of bias in their own interviewing or questionnaire design; they tend to accept everything their volunteers say uncritically; and they set out with a hypothesis that they are determined to *prove*.

It doesn't worry me if Shere Hite wants to make an argument (or write a book) by reprinting letters and drawing elaborate generalizations about all women. She may even be right in her analysis; to say she is writing social science "fiction" doesn't mean her argument is untrue.

What does worry me is the fact that so many media reports regard Hite's methods as *tangential* or amusingly controversial, and that so many journalists reported her findings without knowing her methods. By obscuring the truth that what we know depends on how we know it, social science fiction contributes to the uncritical and mindless attitude that one study is as good as another, that evidence is intellectually unnecessary for one's argument. Most of all, I dislike the trend toward science-coated journalism because it represents yet another domain in this society in which image is everything and substance counts for little. If it looks like science, has numbers like science, and asserts that it is science, it must be science. Why, that's enough these days to make the nightly news.

5
STORIES VERSUS STATISTICS

Argument by anecdote tends to go hand-in-hand with either/or thinking: The story of one patient unfairly confined in a mental institution may persuade us that none should be confined; the story of one ex-mental patient on a rampage may convince us that all people with mental problems should be locked up. Can you think of other dramatic stories in the news that have influenced public opinion on psychological issues? How can research and statistical analysis help us reach informed decisions on such issues and avoid the trap of emotional reasoning and either/or thinking?

Anecdotes: Coat Hangers of Truth

The Los Angeles Times

October 7, 1991

Chances are you don't know anything about Gladys Burr, who made news headlines many years ago. Burr had been involuntarily confined to a mental institution in 1936, with an incorrect diagnosis of mental retardation and psychosis. (Her family didn't want her and had her committed.) In spite of repeated letters to the authorities, no one paid any attention to her requests for freedom for 42 years. "I asked to get out of there so many times," Burr said on her release in 1978, "but they didn't respond, they didn't seem to care."

Today we don't hear about the many Gladys Burrs who were warehoused in institutions without treatment, without legal representation, and with little hope of ever being released. We don't hear anymore about the mentally disturbed individuals who spent far longer in mental hospitals for committing minor crimes than they would have spent in prison. These injustices have been corrected. Today, we hear different stories, about other injustices demanding society's interest.

Thus, in 1985, the same year that Gladys Burr won $235,000 in compensation for her lost life, Sylvia Seegrist went on a murderous spree in a shopping mall, killing two people and wounding eight others with a semiautomatic rifle. Seegrist had been hospitalized 12 times in ten years for violent attacks, and had just been let out after a four-month confinement for stabbing someone. Her parents and psychiatrists had been unable to commit her against her will.

Stories like these are the heart and soul of human life and of the news. We think in stories. We respond emotionally to stories. They enrage, inspire, amuse, and motivate. The case study is an indispensable tool for the psychotherapist, the reporter, the novelist, and the teacher, for it makes dry statistics live and dull theories vivid. This fact of mental life makes it difficult, however, for educators trying to promote critical and scientific thinking. They are forever trying to explain the dangers of arguing by anecdote, of trying to form social policy on the basis of one good story.

We cannot live without stories, but we must do our best to avoid basing law and reforms on them. One person's story may be true, but it is rarely the whole truth and nothing but the truth.

I was thinking of the power of anecdote and of Gladys Burr when I read Dr. George Flesh's essay in this newspaper, misleadingly titled "Why I No Longer Do Abortions." (Actually, he said that he will perform early abortions under certain conditions.) It was a touching personal essay, accompanied by a vivid, emotion-evoking photograph of a fetus. The essay contained several vivid, emotion-evoking anecdotes about women who said they wanted abortions for trivial reasons; they hadn't finished remodeling the kitchen or they wanted a trip to Europe before having a baby. These are the kind of anecdotes that convey the impression that women who have abortions are vain, self-involved, and petty. Why should abortion be legal, if women like that are going to have them?

I don't doubt Flesh's story, which may be true for him, but it is not the whole story. What we no longer see in the media is the kind of essays and photographs that were published in the late 1960s and early 1970s, before Roe vs. Wade. I remember a famous, horrifying photograph of a naked woman, crouched on a bare floor, dead of hemorrhaging from a self-induced abortion. I remember doctors writing essays, as passionate as Flesh's, about why they *would* perform abortions, if the law allowed: so that hospital wards would never again be full of women with perforated uteruses, women recovering or dying from botched illegal or self-administered abortions.

Entire wards were once full of such women. They aren't in hospitals anymore, so we don't have pictures of them.

No social program or law is perfect. Any system we devise to solve a problem will produce people who manipulate it, who cheat, who turn it to their advantage, or who fall through its cracks. Efforts to correct the involuntary confinement of people like Gladys Burr, for example, created problems like the inability to confine people like Sylvia Seegrist. Today, because of legal reforms, it is difficult to hospitalize people involuntarily for longer than a few weeks, even those who are dangerous to themselves or others; it is even difficult to keep patients who want to stay. And so reformers must go back to the drawing board, to think of better ways of protecting the public from people who are dangerously disturbed without forcibly incarcerating people who are not.

Similarly, I have no doubt that some women have abortions for rea-

15

sons other people disapprove of. We will hear these stories as long as abortion is legal. To avoid arguing by anecdote, however, we also must ask about the stories we *aren't* hearing. In the case of abortion, what stories will follow when abortions are illegal?

The answer, throughout history and in every country, has been clear: millions of women will try to have abortions anyway, for reasons of desperation rather than vanity. I realize that anti-abortion activists care less about these women than about the millions of fetuses that are aborted; it is their prerogative to favor the life of the fetus over the life of its mother. For me, it is more significant that every 20 minutes, every day of the year, somewhere in the world a woman dies having an illegal abortion. That is not an anecdote; it's a statistic, the kind of evidence on which issues, especially emotional issues, should be decided.

6
ILLUSORY CORRELATIONS

Pornography is one of those social issues that often elicits simplistic and emotional reasoning, partly because of conflicts over what, exactly, it is. If you were a social scientist, how would you go about designing an experiment to find out whether pornography contributes to antisocial behavior, as many of its critics claim it does? Who would serve as your subjects—convicted criminals or everyday law-abiding folks? How would you define "pornography": as any graphic portrayal of sex, as sex involving violence, as sex that degrades women (and how, but the way, would you define "degrading"?), or as something else? What kind of pornography would you use? What would be your measure of "antisocial behavior," and what kind of control group would you need? Most important: How might your definition of pornography and your own emotional reactions to sexually explicit material influence your findings?

The Illogic of Linking Pornography and Rape

The Los Angeles Times

July 7, 1986

Attention, students of Statistics 101. Here is your final exam. It consists of two questions:

1. If 100 police officers testify that every drug addict they arrested was found to have milk in the refrigerator at home, why can't we conclude that drinking milk leads to drug addiction?
2. If 100 women testify that the men who raped them had read pornographic magazines, why can't we conclude that pornography causes rape?

Give yourself five points if you realize that both faulty conclusions ignore the negative cases: the many children who drink milk and do not become drug addicts, the many men (and women) who read pornography and do not become rapists and child molesters.

Give yourself ten points if you also answered that links between events do not tell us anything about which event causes which. As statisticians say, "Correlation is not causation." Even if drug addicts turn out (in controlled studies) to be unusually fond of milk, we cannot conclude that drinking milk *causes* drug abuse. Perhaps drugs create a desire for milk. Even if rapists are unusually fond of pornography, we cannot conclude that pornography causes rape. Perhaps rapists are men who are drawn to pornographic literature. Or perhaps a third factor, such as physical abuse in childhood, causes men to rape *and* to enjoy violent pornography.

17

These lessons in statistical reasoning were entirely overlooked by the [1986] Meese Commission on Pornography. The basic research question—does pornography cause people (mostly men) to abuse, rape, and exploit others (mostly women)?—was never satisfactorily answered by the commission. It could not have been. The commission members, like their predecessors in Richard Nixon's era, didn't even agree on what pornography is.

Among the members of the commission who dissented from its main report were Judith Becker, a behavioral scientist whose career has been devoted to evaluating and treating the victims and perpetrators of sexual crimes, and Ellen Levine, [then] the editor of *Women's Day* magazine. They argued that the short time and the limited funds that had been granted to the commission meant that a "full airing of the differences" among its members, much less the issuing of a comprehensive report, was impossible. As a result, they concluded, "No self-respecting investigator would accept conclusions based on such a study." Among their objections:

• No effort was made to procure an accurate sample of the varieties and distribution of pornography; visual materials "were skewed to the very violent and extremely degrading." For that matter, portrayals of the violent degradation of women were limited to pornographic films; horror films and contemporary popular films that portray gruesome violence against women were ignored.

• Little effort was made to acquire testimony from people who enjoy pornography and are not harmed by it. It would not have been easy to get such testimony, but not because it doesn't exist. The commission members were understandably sympathetic toward the victims of sexual crimes who tearfully testified that their abusers loved pornography, but our social climate does not encourage the millions of consumers of X-rated films, soft-core magazines, and Victorian erotica to freely admit that they enjoy it.

• Social science studies have been conducted mostly on male college student volunteers; their results cannot be extrapolated to sex offenders or any other group.

The dissenters concluded: "To say that exposure to pornography in and of itself causes an individual to commit a sexual crime is simplistic, not supported by the social science data, and overlooks many of the other variables that may be contributing causes." Yet the commission's findings will provide an excuse to do what the commission was determined to do from the outset: harass and intimidate purveyors and purchasers of pornography, whatever that is.

Becker told me about a discussion that members of the commission were having about "victims of pornography." At last she asked, "What, exactly, is a victim of pornography?"

The commission members struggled to answer. "Someone who has been raped," one member said. "That is a victim of the crime of rape," another replied. "Someone whose father or brother abused her." "That is a victim of incest."

After more than an hour of these exchanges, Becker finally concluded that a "victim of pornography" is "someone who sustains a paper cut while turning the pages of a sex magazine." There is no better, and no more scientific, definition than that one. Until there is, the government would do well to prosecute people who commit crimes of violence against either sex, and stay out of the mind-control business.

7

THINKING CRITICALLY ABOUT ALTERNATIVE MEDICINE

The field of "alternative" medicine often provokes either-or thinking on a national scale: If you are ill, either you seek traditional medicine (prescription drugs, surgery, invasive tests) or you seek alternatives (herbal remedies, meditation, acupuncture, and the like). What is a better, more constructive way to think about the contributions and limitations of both approaches? Why, given the astonishing successes of traditional medicine in prolonging life and in eradicating such killer diseases as polio and smallpox, are so many people disenchanted with it?

Review of *The Alternative Medicine Handbook: The Complete Reference Guide to Alternative and Complementary Therapies*
By Barrie Cassileth
W. W. Norton, 1998

Skeptic Magazine, November 1998, by Carol Tavris and Avrum Bluming

In our respective capacities as a social psychologist (CT) and a physician (AB), we encounter the public hunger for non-traditional approaches to medical care with growing frequency. At dinner parties, on planes, and at conferences, in the privacy of a visit over tea or an office consultation, people want to tell us about their successes with alternative therapies—homeopathy, crystals, vitamins, enzymes, Rolfing, acupuncture, shark cartilage treatments, biofeedback, and countless others. Recently, one of us met a famous entertainer who sang the praises of chelation therapy, the intravenous injection of certain chemicals into the bloodstream that supposedly cause the excretion of harmful minerals, arterial plaque, and other bad stuff.

Once thought to be the exclusive domain of the charlatan and the gullible minority, these alternative treatments are now referred to, collectively, as Complementary and Alternative medicine (CAM), and their influence has oozed from the tabloids and talk shows into the examining rooms of even the most sophisticated medical centers.

The movement to promote CAM is driven by twin engines: the aggressive marketing of health-oriented commercial companies; and the demands of patients searching for cures for everything from normal malaises to life-threatening diseases.

Ironically, public support for unscientific and as-yet unvalidated cures has risen in direct response to the stunning success of scientific research in this century, research that has virtually eradicated many devastating killers, including smallpox, polio, and diphtheria. The public, whose expectations of health and longevity were raised by science, is now exasperated that science can't fix *everything*. And so it seeks alternatives. In 1990, according to one team of investigators, the number of visits to providers of unconventional therapy in the U.S. had exceeded the number of visits to all primary care physicians.

And yet, of course, the public is on to something. Some alternative treatments and psychological interventions, such as biofeedback, hypnosis, and meditation, are demonstrably effective for certain problems. Others, such as aromatherapy and our own personal favorite, humor therapy, couldn't hurt; they sure make you *feel* better, whether you *get* better or not. And some are flat-out frauds that can cost money and lives.

What is needed, therefore, is a consumer guide, and Barrie Cassileth's *The Alternative Medicine Handbook* is a good one. Cassileth has the experience for this task; she is affiliated with the schools of medicine at Harvard and Duke, is a founding member of the Advisory Council to the NIH Office of Alternative Medicine, and has published extensively on this subject in peer-reviewed medical journals, including the *New England Journal of Medicine.*

Cassileth takes on a broad range of material, divided into seven sections: routes to health and spiritual fulfillment (e.g., homeopathy, acupuncture, naturopathic medicine); dietary and herbal remedies (e.g., fasting, herbal medicine, spiritual fulfillment, macrobiotics, vegetarianism); mental techniques (e.g., biofeedback, hypnosis, meditation); alternative biological treatments (e.g., cell therapy, colon/detoxification therapies, shark cartilage); reducing pain and stress through bodywork (e.g., Rolfing, Tai Chi, chiropractic, massage); enhancing well-being through the senses (aromas, art, dance, humor, light, music); and external energy forces (e.g., crystal healing, prayer, shamanism, therapeutic touch).

For each treatment, she provides a capsule summary of its history, basic justifications, therapeutic claims, an analysis of any research-based evidence for its efficacy, and an address for additional information. Cassileth's balanced approach will, we think, appeal both to skeptics who just want the data and to believers who don't want to be made to feel like fools for wishing to experiment with some appealing but unvalidated method. She has a calm and reassuring tone, explaining just what the adherents of some therapy claim, whether the therapy appears to be safe, whether it might have possible benefits, and what its known dangers are.

For example, in discussing herbal remedies and nutritional supplements,

Cassileth notes that few physicians and patients are aware that the Dietary Supplement and Health Education Act of 1994 removed these products from FDA review. As a consequence, she cautions, they are no longer evaluated for either safety or purity, nor are they studied to determine if they support a promoter's claims. Some products contain none of their advertised components. Further, labels on these products rarely include information about the risks, side effects, or possible harmful interactions with other substances. This lack of federal oversight is now under review.

On the other hand, one of us (CT) was happy to learn that massage, her own stress-reducer of choice, is definitely beneficial, not only mentally but physically, because it brings fresh oxygen to body tissues, rids overworked muscles of excess lactic acid, and improves circulation. The other of us (AB), wouldn't submit to a massage by a person not his wife if you paid him cash money, but that's his problem.

Many people who are attracted to CAM claim proudly that they are being open-minded; but as philosopher Carlye Marney cautioned, "A window stuck open is as useless as a window stuck closed. In either case, you've lost the use of the window." Scientists, physicians, and skeptics owe the public an open mind, a critical eye, and the understanding that in science there are no facts, there are only interpretations. Cassileth's book offers exactly the right combination of open mind and critical eye.

Oh, yes, about that entertainer who spends $100 a month on Chelation Therapy: We looked it up, and learned that chelation "has been a proven treatment for lead and other heavy-metal poisoning for over half a century"— and that's all it's known to be useful for. Claims that it is effective for thyroid disorders, high cholesterol, hardening of the arteries, cancer, Alzheimer's disease, diabetes, and countless other ailments, or that it is an effective and less invasive alternative to coronary bypass surgery and angioplasty, are totally unsupported. And one more thing: It can have toxic effects, including kidney and bone marrow damage, irregular heart rhythm, inflammation of the veins, and even death. As in all things, *caveat emptor.*

8

THINKING CRITICALLY ABOUT MYSTICAL MESSAGES

If you were the parent of an autistic or retarded child, you might be vulnerable to programs that claimed to be able to help your child communicate with you via an adult "facilitator." If you were a farmer struggling to survive during a drought, you might welcome anyone who claimed to be able to help you find underground sources of water by using dowsing rods. If you watched someone in a trance engaging in "automatic writing"—producing words that appear to come from a spirit rather than from the person—you might become convinced of the existence of ghosts. The book discussed in this review is a model of critical thinking about "mystical messages," whether conveyed through dowsers, Ouija boards, automatic writing, or supposed "facilitators" for autistic children. What is the emotional appeal of these practices? What is a more logical and valid explanation of what is really going on in each case?

Review of *Nonconscious Movements: From Mystical Messages to Facilitated Communication*
By Herman H. Spitz
Lawrence Erlbaum Associates, 1997

The American Journal of Mental Retardation, September 1998

For many years, Herman H. Spitz has been investigating claims of new pedagogical and psychological methods for raising the intelligence of people with mental retardation. "Alas," he writes, "I found no magic cures; what I found instead was an astonishing variety of human behavior on the part of those making the claims, ranging from outright fraud to honest self-deception." When facilitated communication (FC) came along, Spitz recognized another "popular delusion [that] was happening not in the past but right before our eyes, presenting an opportunity not to be missed." Spitz recognized that the basis of FC was the simple, universal, but widely misunderstood phenomenon of involuntary muscle movement—in this case, the unconscious movement of the "facilitator's" hand over that of the child with autism.

Involuntary (unconscious) muscle movements are ubiquitous and normal; they are essential to survival. You couldn't live a day if your conscious mind had to process all the things your body is doing at any given moment: uncrossing your legs so your knee doesn't go numb, adjusting your shoulders while you sit at the computer, waving your hands to emphasize an argument, nodding your head ever so slightly (or shaking it in disapproval) while you listen to a friend's latest adventures, driving the car while your mind worries about a deadline. Many nonconscious movements are minute, even unobservable: a dowsing rod eventually bends down not because it has found water, but because the hand holding the rod becomes fatigued. Likewise, Clever Hans, the turn-of-the-century "thinking horse" who allegedly had astonishing mathematical talents, was a clever horse, all right, but not at math. He was clever at reading the slight involuntary head movements his human observers made when he pawed the right answer.

We are so oblivious to most of our physical movements, especially when our attention is diverted elsewhere, Spitz argues, that many people refuse to believe they occur at all; or they ascribe these movements to "other worldly beings or to mysterious forces that have escaped scientific scrutiny." When facilitators deny that they are influencing the responses of autistic children, Spitz notes, they aren't lying; they really believe it. Likewise, he notes, "Automatic script writers, Ouija board users, and facilitators do not consciously know what they write and deny that they are directing the writing. Pendulum holders reject the idea that they move the pendulum and dowsers that they move the branch. Table movers believe that they follow, not move, the table. Mind-readers make use of the fact that their guides unwittingly generate muscle movements that can be read by a sensitive and skillful muscle reader. . . . These follies never end."

Spitz sets out to understand the reasons that most facilitators refuse to believe that they are unwittingly guiding their partners, and the reasons that the people who promote FC continue to deny the clear objective evidence that the method is a sham. His quest takes him on an enlightening examination of FC's all-too-numerous historical and contemporary relatives: the many delusions and outright hoaxes that have been perpetrated by people who fail to recognize (or who intentionally disregard evidence of) the ubiquity of nonconscious movements.

Nonconscious Movements examines various phenomena produced by involuntary muscle movements: facilitated communication; a history of Clever Hans and Lady the Wonder Horse, who supposedly could receive messages telepathically; and mind-reading, table moving, dowsing, Ouija boards, and automatic handwriting. Spitz reviews the normal cognitive processes that make people receptive to beliefs in FC and its relatives, including the self-fulfilling prophecy, cognitive dissonance, and the biases of self-deception.

Spitz devotes a chapter to exploring the possible reasons for the alarming number of false allegations of sexual abuse that facilitators have communicated. What, he asks, is going on in the conscious and unconscious motivations of the facilitators who

24

make up unfounded charges of sexual abuse? Spitz considers "surface" explanations, based on behavioral principles such as reinforcements, as well as "depth" explanations, based on nonconscious motivations.

Some facilitators, he believes, are driven by motives that are hardly mysterious: Making dramatic accusations through the method of FC gives them a means of controlling others, exacting revenge on parents and colleagues (via accusations supposedly made by the autistic child), and getting attention and power. Other facilitators, he believes, may be releasing the "conflicting and troubling feelings that resulted from their own abuse." And many are acting out a self-fulfilling prophecy; in their training, many facilitators are actually told to expect their students to raise charges of abuse.

In spite of the mountain of empirical evidence that has discredited it, Spitz warns, FC "continues to spread like a virus run rampant." Its proponents don't back down because they are eager to protect their livelihoods, reputations, and self-esteem, and undoubtedly too because they are scared to face the disappointment and wrath (not to mention lawsuits) of parents and educators if they say, "we were wrong."

These vested interests and face-saving denials of incontrovertible evidence are the reason, Spitz correctly observes, that further research discrediting FC "will simply fall on deaf ears." Precisely, which is why it is so important for the rest of us to be listening. Spitz's book is important because students and professionals alike need to be reminded that FC is only the latest, but not the last, in a long line of hoaxes, to which we are all vulnerable if we do not use reason and evidence to counterbalance our human longing for easy cures, quick fixes, and miracles.

PART II

CONTROVERSIES IN CHILD DEVELOPMENT

Nothing a mother does is considered right?

9
THE WORKING MOTHER DEBATE

The history of advice to mothers might be summarized as: You need help because you don't know what you're doing; and whatever you do, it will probably be wrong and your child will end up blaming you. Why does the specific content of advice to mothers keep changing? How do economic developments in the larger culture, such as a need for women's participation in the labor force, affect that advice? What is wrong with the familiar questions "Should mothers work?" and "Is day-care harmful to children?" What other questions could we be asking?

Review of *A Mother's Place:
Taking the Debate About Working Mothers Beyond
Guilt and Blame*
By Susan Chira
HarperCollins, 1998

The New York Times Book Review,
May 3, 1998

Although I am not an expert on motherhood, I am an expert on motherhood books. I have lived long enough to witness about a dozen cycles of contradictory advice—work/don't work; day care is good/day care is bad; don't work for the child's first six months/six years/lifetime—that clarify one's perspective on the mom business wonderfully.

But it's also why reading Susan Chira's splendid book was both pleasing and depressing. Pleasing, because Chira, the deputy foreign editor of *The New York Times*, makes an eloquent, well-documented case that motherhood does not require martyr-dom and self-obliteration; that motherhood and outside work are not only compatible but also beneficial to mothers and children; that day care does not harm children (on the contrary, it often improves their social and intellectual skills); and that much of what passes as "expert advice" is biased opinion, which is why it changes so rapidly with changing political climates and economic conditions.

A Mother's Place is depressing, however, because it made me feel like Rip Van Winkle, awakening to the exact same arguments about working mothers that modern feminists were raising in the 1970s and that *their* predecessors were in the 1920s. Do we really need to be shown again that time spent with children is not the ultimate measure of good motherhood? That stay-at-home mothers who are bored, resentful, punitive, depressed, or anxious about finances aren't going to be so great for their kids? It seems so.

The need for this book means that one of the most important messages of contemporary feminism and decades-old research in the social sciences has yet to penetrate even the skin of American culture: namely, that a mother's working does not, in and of itself, harm children. A woman (or, increasingly, a man) may want to stay home and watch the children develop; she (or he) may want to give up the corporate rat race. But this decision is a matter of preference, not a requirement for raising healthy children. Yet this preference is supported by a society that is still deeply suspicious of mothers who wish to work, need to work, or, God help them, love to work.

Chira wrote this book, she says, because she kept hearing "that what I wanted was impossible—to be serious about both my work and motherhood." In the 1960s, women began to dispute the "cult of domesticity" of the 1950s, vigorously advocating that women could and should do both. That was news then. By the 1980s, after the mass influx of women into the labor market, the news was the women who were giving up their careers. Today the new news (again) is that women can combine work and motherhood. Chira's book, along with *The Sacrificial Mother*, by Carin Rubenstein, and *When Mothers Work*, by Joan K. Peters, is part of the latest turn of the wheel.

This endless debate about "a mother's place" could occur only in a culture that gives mothers no help, provides no universal and reliable system of day care, and then blames mothers for whatever they do: work (if they are middle-class), not work (if they are on welfare), work too much (if they are ambitious), or work too little (if they aren't ambitious enough and gutlessly take the "mommy track").

I mustn't be too irritable, though, about women's continual rediscovery of the mother-work dilemma. Motherhood, like illness, is another country: If you haven't been there, you can't quite imagine it. You can read about it, sympathize with those who have crossed the border, fume about the inherent unfairness of its burdens, but nothing takes the place of experience. That is why childless women can delusionally believe that having children won't affect their lives. And it is why they desperately start looking to experts for help once actual children arrive.

So, setting aside my sense of déjà vu when reading Chira's book, I wholeheartedly recommend it to politicians, pediatricians, fathers, and especially working mothers who feel buffeted by incessant criticism. These are perilous times for mothers who work outside the home, as revealed by the speed with which the trial of Louise Woodward, the au pair found guilty of the death of Matthew Eappen, was transformed into a trial of the baby's mother.

The national antipathy toward Deborah Eappen for having the

temerity to work—even if it was only three days a week, even if she came home for lunch, even if she taught her au pairs CPR and child-care skills—is reflected, Chira demonstrates, in custody decisions nationwide. Judges routinely reward fathers who take any part in child rearing, and they routinely punish mothers who aren't home with the kids full time. Of course, staying home often means a mother doesn't have money to contest an ex-husband who sues for custody on the grounds that he earns more money than she does. And it often means that women won't have enough money in Social Security or pension plans to provide for their old age. But, hey, aren't women supposed to be self-sacrificing?

Chira's book is a harmonious blend of her own experiences, interviews and research. Her concerns about leaving her children in the care of others, her jealousy when her children turn to their father instead of to her for comfort, and her insecurity about how to balance work demands with those of her family will resonate with many women. She wittily dissects the baby-care advice biz, pointing out the stay-at-home bias of modern gurus such as Penelope Leach. And she highlights what social science has reliably indicated for years: that there is no one right way to be a mother, that kids do fine as long as they get love and attention, and that parents are not the sole influence on their children, regardless of how much time and money parents lavish on them.

As Chira shows in her brilliant last chapter, "Reimagining Motherhood," it is time to drop that tired, unanswerable question—"does working harm children?"—and move to the more important one: How can we make sure it doesn't? It is time to replace "does day care harm children?" with efforts to make child care available to all who need it. Until we do, mothers will continue to feel defensive about the choices they make and blame those who make different ones. Who benefits from this division among women, and from blaming women for whatever choice they make? Those who want women out of the workplace and out of politics. Who loses? Everyone.

you have to have peace . . . inner self

10

HOW MUCH INFLUENCE DO MOTHERS HAVE?

How would you define the qualities and behaviors involved in being a good mother? Are they different from those you would apply to being a good father? And how about asking a more radical question entirely: Do mothers, "good" or "bad," have the primary influence on how their children turn out?

Even Moms Can't Guarantee a Perfect Life

The Los Angeles Times

May 10, 1998

You might think that women would be more relaxed about mothering these days. All they'd have to do is notice that expert advice changes as often as hemlines and hairstyles: Pick up the baby/let the baby cry; sleep with the baby/don't sleep with the baby; feed the baby on demand/feed the baby at rigid intervals.

But women are insecure because there is no commonly accepted idea of what it means to be a good mother. Fathers have it easier in this regard; they just have to show up and they are automatically considered "good," whereas mothers are always trying to prove to themselves and the world that they aren't "bad." If a woman works outside the home, she's depriving her children of her constant attention (which is bad), but if she stays home, she's smothering her children with constant attention (which also is bad). If she's middle class, working is

extremely bad, but if she's poor, not working is extremely bad.

In some ways, things are getting worse. Years ago, a woman was allowed five years to mold her child's personality. According to Freud, after the first five "formative years" ended in the crisis of the Oedipal complex, the child's personality was set for life. Today, however, some psychologists tell mothers that the first three years of life are the most important, while others think that all critical events happen during the first year. Indeed, after some highly publicized studies of infant "bonding" after birth, it seemed that a mother had only five minutes in which to make or break her child's destiny.

Likewise, when researchers announced what most mothers have always known—that babies aren't passive little blobs but active learners from the beginning—you could hear the alarms across the land. Although the alarms need only have sounded for children completely deprived of intellectual stimulation and cuddling, middle-class parents overreacted. Is stimulation good? Then we'll make sure our child is stimulated every waking moment. Is cuddling good? Then we'll never put that baby down. Is talking to the baby good? Excellent, we'll make sure the baby hears lots of English, Spanish, and Japanese.

Ironically, this panic about doing the right thing to produce the perfect child is probably the worst thing for the child and the parent. Research in developmental psychology ought to help parents relax. Here's why.

First, it is not harmful to children if their mothers work. Mothers who obliterate their own needs and abilities for the sake of their children do not benefit their children, their marriages, or themselves.

Second, there is no key moment or stage in early childhood in which a child's destiny is determined forever. Obviously it's good to give children stimulation and cuddling from the start, but one wrong step will not doom the child to trauma. Children are more resilient than that.

For instance, longitudinal studies find that with adequate love and support, most children overcome even extraordinary hardships, including having been born to drug-addicted mothers, parental alcoholism, homelessness, and war. Although we are told repeatedly that abused children inevitably grow up to be abusers, the fact is that while being abused increases the risk, more than 70 percent of abused children do not become abusive parents.

Conversely, research also finds that some children who have had the best parental care and guidance later succumb to drugs, addiction, mental illness, or violence. Parents simply cannot control all the possible paths their children may take. Between the parents' best efforts and the resulting child lie other factors: the child's temperament, genetically influenced dispositions and vulnerabilities, experiences outside the family (especially with peers), and the child's perceptions of events. Parents can help a temperamentally shy child learn to cope better in situations that make the child anxious, but they aren't going to turn her into Bette Midler.

Of course, many parents are understandably worried about protecting their children and making sure their children have every advantage in today's complex world. The news is full of stories about children who kill, teenagers on drugs, and sadistic day-care workers. But the statistical reality—that violence is declining, that the vast majority of teenagers who experiment with drugs never become addicts or drug abusers, that cruel day-care workers are rarer than cruel parents—is not as compelling as the horrifying scare story.

All parents worry; that goes with the job description. But it's time to put matters in perspective. There is no one right way to be a good mother and no secret formula for raising a perfect child. And no one can give parents the guarantee they want most; that their child will be safe from life, for life.

So I propose a moratorium on mother-blaming and mother-guilt. You can do all the right things and your kid will blame you anyway, and you can do all the wrong things, and your kid, amazingly, will muddle through.

11

HOW MUCH INFLUENCE DO PARENTS HAVE?

If ever a book challenged the fundamental assumptions of researchers in the field of child development, this one is it. The Nurture Assumption invited open-minded readers to examine their own prejudices about parents' power to determine how their children turn out. How much influence do parents really have on their children's abilities, personalities, and experiences? As you read this review, ask yourself whether your own reactions to this question are based on anecdotes about your own life, your personal feelings about whether you want the argument to be true or false, or the strength (or weakness) of the evidence. Why do you think people reacted so emotionally to this book?

Review of *The Nurture Assumption: Why Children Turn Out the Way They Do*
By Judith Rich Harris
The Free Press, 1998

The New York Times Book Review,
September 13, 1998

As I was writing this review, two friends called to ask me about "that book that says parents don't matter." Well, that's not what it says. What *The Nurture Assumption* does say about parents and children, however, warrants the lively controversy it began generating even before publication.

Judith Rich Harris was chucked out of graduate school at Harvard on the grounds that she was unlikely to become a proper experimental psychologist. She never became an academic and instead turned her hand to writing textbooks in developmental psychology. From this bird's-eye vantage point, she began to question widespread belief in the "nurture assumption—the notion that parents are the most important part of a child's environment and can determine, to a large extent, how the child turns out." She believes that parents must share credit (or blame) with the child's own temperament, and, most of all with the child's peers. "The world that children share with their peers is what shapes their behavior and modifies the characteristics they were born with," Harris writes, "and hence determines the sort of people they will be when they grow up."

The public may be forgiven for saying, "Here we go again." One year we're told bonding is the key, the next

34

that it's birth order. Wait, what really matters is stimulation. The first five years of life are the most important; no, the first three years; no, it's all over by the first year. Forget that: It's all genetics! Cancel those baby massage sessions!

What makes Harris's book important is that it puts all these theories into larger perspective, showing what each contributes and where it is flawed. Some critics may pounce on her for not having a Ph.D. or an academic position, and others will quarrel with the importance she places on peers and genes, but they cannot fault her scholarship. Harris is not generalizing from a single study that can be attacked on statistical grounds, or even from a single field; she draws on research from behavior genetics (the study of genetic contributions to personality), social psychology, child development, ethology, evolution, and culture. Lively anecdotes about real children suffuse this book, but Harris never confuses anecdotes with data. The originality of *The Nurture Assumption* lies not in the studies she cites, but in the way she has reconfigured them to explain findings that have puzzled psychologists for years.

First, researchers have been unable to find any child-rearing practice that predicts children's personalities, achievements, or problems outside the home. Parents don't have a single child-rearing style anyway, because how they treat their children depends largely on what the children are like. They are more permissive with easy children and more punitive with defiant ones.

Second, even when parents do treat their children the same way, the children turn out differently. The majority of children of troubled and even abusive parents are resilient and do not suffer lasting psychological damage. Conversely, many children of the kindest and most nurturing parents succumb to drugs, mental illness, or gangs.

Third, there is no correlation—zero—between the personality traits of adopted children and their adoptive parents or other children in the home, as there should be if "home environment" had a strong influence.

Fourth, how children are raised—in day care or at home, with one parent or two, with gay parents or straight ones, with an employed mom or one who stays home—has little or no influence on children's personalities.

Finally, what parents do with and for their children affects children mainly when they are with their parents. For instance, mothers influence their children's play only while the children are playing with them; when the child is playing alone or with a playmate, it makes no difference what games were played with mom.

Most psychologists have done what anyone would do when faced with this astonishing, counterintuitive evidence: They have tried to dismiss it. Yet eventually the most unlikely idea wins if it has the evidence to back it up. As Carole Wade, a behavioral scientist, puts it, trying to squeeze existing facts into an outdated theory is like trying to fit a double-sized sheet onto a queen-sized bed.

One corner fits, but another pops out. You need a new sheet or a new bed.

The Nurture Assumption is a new sheet, one that covers the discrepant facts. I don't agree with all the author's claims and interpretations; often she reaches too far to make her case, throwing the parent out with the bath water, as it were. But such criticisms should not detract from her accomplishment, which is to give us a richer, more accurate portrait of how children develop than we have had from outdated Freudianism or piecemeal research.

The first problem with the nurture assumption is nature. The findings of behavior genetics show, incontrovertibly, that many personality traits and abilities have a genetic component. No news here; many others have reported this research, notably the psychologist Jerome Kagan in *The Nature of the Child*. But genes explain only about half of the variation in people's personalities and abilities. What's the other half?

Harris's brilliant stroke was to change the discussion from nature (genes) and nurture (parents) to its older version: heredity and environment. "Environment" is broader than nurture. Children, like adults, have two environments: their homes and their world outside the home; their behavior, like ours, changes depending on the situation they are in. Many parents know the eerie experience of having their child's teacher describe their child in terms they barely recognize (*"my* kid did *what?"*). Children who fight with their siblings may be placid with friends. They can be honest at home and deceitful at school, or vice versa. At home children learn how their parents want them to behave and what they can get away with; but, Harris shows, "These patterns of behavior are not like albatrosses that we have to drag along with us wherever we go, all through our lives. We don't even drag them to nursery school."

Harris has taken a factor, peers, that everyone acknowledges is important, but instead of treating it as a nuisance in children's socialization, she makes it a major player. Children are merciless in persecuting a kid who is different—one who says "Warshington" instead of "Washington," one who has a foreign accent or wears the wrong clothes. (Remember?) Parents have long lamented the apparent cruelty of children and the obsessive conformity of teen-agers, but, Harris argues, they have missed the point: Children's attachment to their peer groups is not irrational, it's essential. It is evolution's way of seeing to it that kids bond with each other, fit in, and survive. Identification with the peer group, not identification with the parent, is the key to human survival. That is why children have their own traditions, words, rules, games; their culture operates in opposition to adult rules. Their goal is not to become successful adults but successful children. Teen-agers want to excel as teen-agers, which means being unlike adults.

It has been difficult to tease apart the effects of parents and peers, Harris observes, because children's environments often duplicate parental values, language, and customs. (Indeed, many parents see to it that they do.) To see what factors are strongest, therefore, we must look at situations in which these environments clash. For example, when parents value academic achievement and a student's peers do not, who wins? Typically, peers. Differences between black and white teenagers in achievement have variously been attributed to genes or single mothers, but differences vanish when researchers control for the peer group: whether its members value achievement and expect to go to college, or regard academic success as a hopeless dream or sellout to "white" values.

Are there exceptions? Of course, and Harris anticipates them. Some children in anti-intellectual peer groups choose the lonely path of nerdy devotion to schoolwork. And some have the resources, from genes or parents, to resist peer pressure. But exceptions should not detract from the rule: that children, like adults, are oriented to their peers. Do you dress, think, and behave more like others of your generation, your parents, or the current crop of adolescents?

Harris writes beautifully, in a tone both persuasive and conversational. But many people are deeply invested, financially and emotionally, in the "nurture assumption" and won't give it up, I suspect, without a fight: the vast advice-to-parents industry and the "guilty mother" brigade, whose work fills our airwaves, books, magazines, and newspapers; therapists who believe that our personalities and problems are created by unconscious dynamics, neurotic parents, or childhood experiences; politicians elected on the claims that day care, divorce, and working mothers are bad for children; people who want to blame their parents for everything that's wrong in their lives; and parents who understandably want credit for their efforts to raise good kids in tough times.

Others, however, may reject this book because of concerns about its potential misuses. If children "naturally" exclude "outsiders," why should schools make any effort to integrate children of different ethnicities, sexes, or abilities? Why should we pay for prenatal care or better schools if smart, resilient kids will turn out all right whatever we do, and troubled ones will be lost to deviant peer groups?

These concerns are especially important in our antichild culture, which already lags behind European nations in measures supporting children's health, education, and universal day care. Some people may indeed try to use Harris's evidence to legitimize our national neglect of children. For those committed to the well-being of all children, however, here is information that can lead to better programs, ones that might actually work.

For example, Harris makes it clear why most bilingual education programs have failed: Children will speak the way their friends do. If other kids are speaking the language they hear at home, that's what they'll speak. If other kids speak English with a Spanish or Bostonian accent, they will acquire an accent too. If other kids are speaking a language they don't know, they'll learn it fast. Any program, bilingual or monolingual, that doesn't take into account the power of peers is doomed. Likewise, Harris shows why the costly programs designed to get teenagers to avoid drugs, stay in school, or abstain from sex have been such duds; they have been targeted to individual teen-agers or their parents.

The greatest fear surrounding Harris's book is that her message will somehow encourage the neglect or outright abuse of children. This concern reveals, perhaps, what a deeply antichild culture we are, for it assumes that we are nice to children only out of a desire to make them perfect replicas of ourselves—and if we can't, we might as well abandon them. But if you realize that you can't turn your shy child into an extrovert, does that mean you won't help her cope in scary new situations? Why should the good news that most children are resilient be construed in any way as an endorsement of neglecting their health or permitting adults to abuse them?

Harris believes that parents should treat children well for the reason they should be kind to their partners, not in hopes of transforming their personalities or controlling their futures but in hopes of remaining good friends for a lifetime. Parents matter, she says, primarily in determining the kind of relationship they will have with their children—friend-ly or bitter, accepting or adversarial—and how their children feel about them.

Many readers will disagree with Harris's conclusions about the limited influence of parents. Everyone knows people who have spent untold hours with their shy, difficult, or learning-disabled children (genetic predispositions all) and thereby helped their children succeed in their peer groups, school, and life. And everyone has friends whose harsh, unforgiving, or neglectful parents left wounds that still hurt, though these wounds might never be apparent on a personality test.

But it would be a shame if readers get so focused on the degree to which parents matter that they overlook Harris's most important message, which is that parents aren't *all* that matter. This news should reassure people who blame themselves, as society blames them, for their children's problems with drugs, mental illness, or violence. But it may panic parents who are consumed by a near-hysterical passion to control their children's personalities, abilities, careers, safety, and eating habits, and inspire them to start feverishly trying to micromanage their children's peer groups as well. Forget it. "The idea that we can make our children turn out any way we want is an illusion," Harris writes. "You can neither perfect them nor ruin them. They are not yours to perfect or ruin: they belong to tomorrow." In the current cacophony of advice to parents, could any words be wiser?

12
HOW CRITICAL ARE THE FIRST YEARS OF LIFE?

Like The Nurture Assumption *(see Essay 11), the book reviewed in this essay also aimed to shake up some key assumptions held by the developmental-psychology establishment. The author asked some provocative questions: What is the connection, if any, between neural development in the first three years and later intellectual ability? Are those first years crucial, or can interventions later in life be equally powerful? If you are or expect to be a parent, do you think the answers will affect how you treat your baby? Where do you think society's resources should go in order to help disadvantaged children and illiterate adults improve their mental skills?*

Review of *The Myth of the First Three Years: A New Understanding of Early Brain Development and Lifelong Learning*
By John T. Bruer
The Free Press, 1999

The New York Times Book Review,
October 17, 1999

This century began with the ascendancy of the unconscious and it's ending with the ascendancy of the brain. These very different explanations of behavior have two things in common. Both the unconscious and the brain are invisible to the naked eye, therefore requiring phalanxes of experts to explain them. And both notions have been used to serve the deeply held American cultural belief in infant determinism, the idea that the first three years of life determine a child's development and personality.

It was bad enough when parents were told that their baby would form a lifelong unconscious image of them, based on how sensitive they were to the tiny tyrant's every emotional need. Now parents are being told to forget the unconscious and attend to brain wiring. As Rob Reiner's "I Am Your Child" campaign puts it, "The early years last forever." This is because, the public is told, the baby's brain is forming trillions of synapses (connections between nerve cells), many of which have, by puberty, been "pruned away." Enriched environments and mental stimulation are critical to synapse production, and thus to

39

a baby's mental, musical, and artistic abilities. Kindergarten is too late.

In this era of the brain, such an argument is powerful. Do *you* know how many synapses you have? Of course not, but if you're like me you will jump at the chance to add a few more, or at least keep the ones you have. So it's no wonder that millions of parents are panicked. When you could only wreck your child's unconscious, the kid could always go to therapy. But if you miss that critical early period for stimulating your baby's brain, your child might never get to Harvard. As Hillary Rodham Clinton said during the 1997 White House Conference on Early Childhood Development and learning, this emphasis on the brain does "ratchet up the guilt."

That is why *The Myth of the First Three Years* is important. John T. Bruer, the president of the James S. McDonnell Foundation, which supports research on neuroscience and cognition, has written a clear and balanced assessment of what research has and has not discovered about infant brains, one that illuminates the connections between research, political values, and social policy. Among his most important observations are these:

• "Most learning is not subject to critical-period constraints," Bruer writes, "nor confined to windows of opportunity that slam shut." For example, the years roughly until puberty are, in general, crucial for acquiring an unaccented second language. But most people can learn another language and improve their skills at any age.

• The most exciting discoveries in neuroscience are that the brain develops throughout life and that brain structure is continually affected by experience. Neuroscientists once believed that lost neurons could not regenerate; now it turns out that sometimes they can. "The brain is not 'cooked' by age 3 or age 10," Bruer writes. "Our brains remain remarkably plastic and we retain the ability to learn throughout our lives."

• Infants subjected to severe, prolonged deprivation do indeed suffer intellectually, though long-term studies find that many recover from even this poor start. But there is no single, correct way to stimulate a baby in order to produce maximum mental benefits. In those famous rat studies showing the benefits of "enriched" environments, the environments were actually typical of how rats live in the wild. Similarly, the natural environments in which most human babies live provide all the stimulation necessary for normal development.

Bruer's most debatable claim is that the rapid explosion of synapses in infancy is "under genetic, not environmental control." But he is right that "more synapses do not necessarily mean more brainpower" and that the loss of synapses is not a result of inadequate stimulation; it is normal, necessary, and unrelated to brain function. We lose synapses by the fistful by adulthood, but our knowledge and mental abilities continue to expand.

40

As Bruer observes, nowadays everyone feels the need to claim that science is on his or her side. Thus, the "I Am Your Child" campaign claims that "brain science" shows that you should be attentive; read, sing, and talk to your baby; be selective about television; choose good day care. But how much reading and singing? How much attention? Neuroscience is silent.

Of course, the heart of this debate is not about what kind of mobiles middle-class parents should hang over their babies' cribs or whether listening to Mozart increases intelligence (it doesn't). It's about where society's resources should go in helping poor and disadvantaged children. Bruer argues that even the most intensive early-intervention programs, notably the Abecedarian project in North Carolina and the nation-wide Infant Health and Development Program, have had modest effects at best. They do boost school performance, but what matters most seems to be intensive training in academic skills over time. Otherwise, many of the benefits of early intervention wear off by adolescence.

Bruer worries that "the myth of the first three years" will persuade the public and lawmakers that once a child is older than 3, we might as well forget any other programs. According to Bruer, bills to reduce or eliminate support for programs for older children (let alone adults) are already being considered in some states: no point providing literacy and education programs in prisons or the military; no point improving schools; such efforts are too little, too late. What the new brain science really shows is that it's never too late. Brain science can therefore be used to argue both that it's important to give babies a good start *and* that a good start is not enough. It can be used to support programs to help underprivileged babies *and* programs aimed at older children and their unemployed, malnourished, or illiterate parents.

The book has several annoying qualities. It is poorly edited (at least 200 of my synapses were deadened by its repetitive conclusions). It lacks a bibliography, so readers cannot find sources easily or check for important citations without struggling through the inadequate notes. Over all, however, these complaints are like ants at a picnic: nuisances, but they need not detract from the ample food for thought.

41

PART III

THE POLITICS AND SCIENCE OF GENDER RESEARCH

13

ARE MEN AND WOMEN "OPPOSITE SEXES"?

Are men from Mars and women from Venus, as one bestseller of the 1990s would have us believe? This essay urges us to break out of such false dichotomies and consider the "excluded middle," in order to gain a better picture of the way most people actually behave. Why do the media constantly harp on the differences between men and women and ignore the overwhelming evidence of their similarities? Is making women the "superior sex" any better than doing the same for men? Is the gender gap a matter of intellect, emotion, and biology, or of power, experience, and expectation?

Disarmament for the Gender Wars

The Los Angeles Times

March 10, 1992

The gender wars have been heating up again. The drumbeat of news stories about rape, harassment, the glass ceiling, the "gender gap" in politics, and the "housework gap" in the home have inflamed feelings on both sides. Beneath the anger and the jokes, I detect real fear that the situation is getting out of hand; both sexes seem increasingly to feel that there is an unbridgeable chasm between them.

This is no wonder, because we are bombarded constantly with assertions of how different the sexes are. Robert Bly celebrated the archetypal differences between Woman and Man. *Science, Newsweek,* and that scholarly publication *Elle* report that men's and women's brains are specialized for different skills. Biomedical researchers worry about the legions of women who suffer various hormonal "syndromes"; men, apparently, lack hormones and moods. But men have lust: Sociobiologists assert that women are biologically programmed to be sexually passive, faithful, and monogamous, whereas the male is designed for promiscuity and pursuit. And a growing contingent of "cultural feminists" argues that women are naturally more nurturant, moral, peace-loving, and earth-friendly than men. Women, they say, are psychologically wired to be the experts at love and intimacy, whereas men, poor souls, are emotionally repressed louts who fear attachment and wouldn't know a nurturant feeling if it sat on their laps.

Oh, dear. If things are this bad, I guess women had better go on home, where they can cultivate their intuitions and hormones, have several babies, and stop annoying men by trying to be like them. As for help with the babies, forget it, because nurturance doesn't come natural to men. And never mind saving the planet, unless we can somehow confine men on special game preserves.

The way that we think about women and men, how we construe our differences and similarities, is not only a fun topic of conversation and an engrossing academic exercise. It profoundly affects our visions of what is possible for society and for our private lives. The reason that our visions conflict so bitterly today is that society is conflicted over woman's place, a conflict that emerged in its modern form with the industrial revolution. Where once the spheres of men's work and women's work coexisted close to the home, now they split into different orbits: the public world of work for him, the private world of the family for her. Accordingly, women became the love experts and men the experts on everything else.

Wherever the sexes live in separate economic spheres, we can expect scientific efforts to legitimize the idea that men and women are fundamentally opposite because of their hormones, brains, natures, or innermost psyches; therefore any expectation of change is hopeless. This idea routinely erupts with renewed vigor every time women take a significant step outside the private sphere. When women tried to enter universities in the nineteenth century, "science" was quick to assert that education would overheat their brains, destroy their ovaries, and make them infertile.

In fact, the weight of the evidence about the "natures" and capabilities of the sexes falls on the side of how similar they are. When I looked into the research on brains, hormones, mental abilities, skills, moods, sexual desires, feelings of love and connection, grief, moral reasoning, empathy, belligerence, and other traits pertaining to the strengths and foibles of the human condition, what I found overwhelmingly was: There is far more variation within each sex than between them. For example:

• Are men's and women's brains differently wired? One eminent researcher in this field summarized her findings this way: "One must not overlook perhaps the most obvious conclusion, which is that basic patterns of male and female brain asymmetry seem to be more similar than they are different." Of course, everyone overlooked it. The few small studies that find sex differences in the brains of rats and humans make the news, but not the studies that find trivial differences or none at all.

• Is male and female sexuality differently programmed? Sociobiologists say yes, pointing to the promiscuous behavior of the males of many species. But other research has established that in many species, including birds, fish, and mammals, females are as promiscuous as males; indeed, many will have multiple copulations even after they have been impregnated. Just as Darwin's description of the "coy female" and "lustful male" gave a scientific gloss to Victorian courting customs, sociobiological theory about modern sexual relationships serves more to justify existing social rules than to illuminate their origins.

• Are women inherently peaceful, nature-loving, and empathic? Men are indeed far more likely than women to behave aggressively; both sexes fear male violence. Yet it does not follow that women are invariably less likely than men to support war, depersonalize the enemy, and despoil the environment, or more likely than men to live in harmony with their neighbors. The archetypes of Man as Noble Warrior and Woman as Saintly Pacifist compliment both sexes, but history serves up ample evidence of female bellicosity and male pacifism.

Indeed, that is what is wrong with all visions that posit an essential opposition between the sexes: They rest on archetype, not reality. Thinking in opposites leads to what philosophers call "the law of the excluded middle," which is where most men and women fall in terms of their qualities, beliefs, values, and capabilities. The very term "opposite sex" implies an underlying antagonism, the pitting of one side against the other, one way (which is right and healthy) versus the other's way (which is wrong and unhealthy). Framing the issue in polarities, regardless of which pole is valued, sets up false choices: Is it better to be logical or intuitive? Emotional or reasonable? Dependent or autonomous? In truth, we are, and should be, all of the above.

I am hopeful that we can find new pathways through these thickets. There is nothing in our nature or intellect that creates the battle of the sexes; the differences that most trouble us are created by the conditions and experiences of our lives. By understanding the real forces that separate women and men, and those that unite us, perhaps we can find better ways to work together, live together, and develop the society that would benefit us all.

14

THE INTERPRETATION
OF DIFFERENCES, I

Given that most men and women fit "the law of the excluded middle," as described in the previous essay, how can we make sense of the gender differences that keep being reported in the media? This essay and the next one consider this question from two angles. In this essay, you can see that sometimes the existence of "differences" depends on how you define the behavior in question. For example, what does "intimacy" mean? Do women and men differ in their ability to form close friendships or in their notions of what friendship means?

How Friendship Was "Feminized"

The New York Times

May 28, 1997

Once upon a time and not so very long ago, everyone thought that men had the great and true-blue friendships. The cultural references stretched through time and art: Damon and Pythias, Hamlet and Horatio, Butch Cassidy and the Sundance Kid. The Lone Ranger never rode off with anyone but Tonto, and Laurel never once abandoned Hardy in whatever fine mess he got them into.

Male friendships were said to grow from the deep roots of shared experience and faithful camaraderie, whereas women's friendships were portrayed as shallow, trivial, and competitive, like Scarlett O'Hara's with her sisters. Women, it was commonly claimed, would sell each other out for the right guy, and even for a good time with the wrong one.

Some social scientists told us that this difference was hard-wired, a result of our evolutionary history. In the early 1970s, for example, the anthropologist Lionel Tiger argued in *Men in Groups* that "male bonding" originated in prehistoric male hunting groups and was carried on today in equivalent pack-like activities: sports, politics, business, and war.

Apparently, women's evolutionary task of rummaging around in the garden to gather the odd yam or kumquat was a solo effort, so females do not bond in the same way. Women prattle on about their feelings, went the stereotype, but men act.

My, how times have changed. In the 1970s and 1980s, female scholars began to dispel the men-are-better stereotype in all domains and women became the majority of psychothera-

48

pists. The result was a positive reassessment of the qualities associated with women, including a "feminizing" of definitions of intimacy and friendship. Accordingly, female friendships are now celebrated as the deep and abiding ones, based as they are on shared feelings and confidences. Male friendships are scorned as superficial, based as they are on shared interests in sports and drinking beer.

In our psychologized culture, "intimacy" is defined as what many women like to do with their friends: talk, express feelings, and disclose worries. Psychologists, most of whom are good talkers, validate this definition as the true measure of intimacy. For example, in a study of "intimacy maturity" in marriage, researchers equated "most mature" with "most verbally expressive." As a woman, I naturally think this is a perfectly sensible equation, but I also know it is an incomplete one. To label people mature or immature, you also have to know how they actually behave toward others.

What about all the men and women who support their families, put the wishes of other family members ahead of their own, or act in moral and considerate ways when conflicts arise? They are surely mature, even if they are inarticulate or do not express their feelings easily. Indeed, what about all the men and women who define intimacy in terms of deeds rather than words: sharing activities, helping one another, or enjoying companionable silence? Too bad for them. That's a "male" definition, and out of favor in these talky times.

Years ago, my husband had to have some worrisome medical tests, and the night before he was to go to the hospital we went to dinner with one of his best friends who was visiting from England. I watched, fascinated, as male stoicism combined with English reserve produced a decidedly unfemale-like encounter. They laughed, they told stories, they argued about movies, they reminisced. Neither mentioned the hospital, their worries, or their affection for each other. They didn't need to.

It is true that women's style of intimacy has many benefits. A large body of research in health psychology and social psychology finds that women's greater willingness to talk about feelings improves their mental and physical health and makes it easier to ask for help.

But as psychologists like Susan Nolen-Hoeksema have shown, women's fondness for ruminating about feelings can also prolong depression, anxiety, and anger. And it can keep women stuck in bad jobs or relationships, instead of getting out of them or doing what is necessary to make them better.

The validation of women's friendships is timely and welcome, as long as it does not simply invert the stereotype. Playing the women-are-better game is fun, but it blinds us to the universal need for intimacy and the many forms that friendship takes. Maybe men could learn a thing or two about friendship from women. But who is to say that women couldn't learn a thing or two from them in exchange?

15

THE INTERPRETATION
OF DIFFERENCES, II

When most people read about a finding that "women are this" and "men are that," differing in some attitude, ability, or behavior, they often assume the difference must be due to something inherent in the makeup of the sexes. This essay was written during the 1996 presidential election, when an apparent gender gap in voting patterns was in the news, but it invites readers to consider alternative explanations for findings about "gender differences" in other contexts. Why do so many of these differences shrink or expand with changing times and cultural events, for example?

Misreading the Gender Gap

The New York Times

September 17, 1996

Do you know about the gender gap in paranormal beliefs? Women are more likely than men to believe in horoscopes and psychics. People who are unsympathetic to women say it's because women are more gullible or dumber than men; those who are sympathetic to women say it's because women are more open-minded or spiritual than men.

Actually, this gender gap pretty much vanishes when you consider years of education and the number of math and science classes a person has taken. What appears to be a gender gap is in fact a science gap.

Do you know about the gender gap in anger? Men are more likely than women to express anger directly and abusively (except maybe in New York, where everyone ventilates).

The anti-woman reason is that women are sneakier and more manipulative than men; the pro-woman version is that women are kinder and less aggressive than men.

Actually, the gender gap in expressions of anger pretty much vanishes when you consider the status of the people involved. Both sexes tend to be indirect and manipulative when they are angry at someone who has more power than they have—say, bosses and police officers. And both sexes are equally likely to lose their tempers with people who have less power than they have—say, store clerks or children. What appears to be a gender gap is really a power gap.

Now everybody is talking about the gender gap in the current Presidential campaign. Why are women, even suburban women, who tend to vote Republican, so much more likely than men to support President Clinton than Bob Dole? According to a New York Times/CBS News poll, women prefer Mr. Clinton over Mr. Dole by 61 percent to 33 percent. Men favor Mr. Clinton, but by a narrower margin: 49 percent to 42 percent.

First, it's interesting that the fluctuating political differences between the sexes, which ranged from trivial in the Nixon-Kennedy election in 1960 to significant today, capture the public imagination in ways that other "gaps"—as in wealth or geographical region—do not. The last time the country became as exercised about opinions divided along other than gender lines was in the days of the "generation gap" during the Vietnam War.

Men and women are not different species and do not come from different planets. The overlap between them, on voting choices or personality traits, is always greater than the differences that make headlines.

Nevertheless, why do more women than men support President Clinton? Conservative explanations, such as one offered by Irving Kristol in *The Wall Street Journal*, are that women "tend to be more sentimental, more risk-averse and less competitive than men . . . and therefore are less inclined to be appreciative of free-market economics."

In short, they are by nature soft-headed liberals—the kind, he added, who devised and continue to support the American welfare state, which "has had a feminine coloration from the very beginning." (I guess the Depression didn't affect men, who must have stood idly by, cheering for free-market economics, while legions of women instituted the New Deal.)

Fortunately for conservatives, most women marry and have children, a condition that apparently neutralizes their inherent sentimentality and turns many of them into proper tough-minded Republicans.

Conservatives are so worried about all those women supporting the Democrats that they are claiming the Democratic Party itself has become "feminized"—just about the nastiest charge they could level at an enemy. The charge not only calls the enemy a wimp; it dismisses as trivial any issues the opposition endorses, such as the right to abortion, government programs for children and the poor, family leave, or gun control, because these "feminine" concerns are of no relevance to the standard-issue human being, that is, the male variety.

Your true Masculinized Republican regards government support of just about any kind as crutches for the whiny. "If terrible things happen to innocent people," Mr. Kristol explains, it's not up to government to help; the poor need only stoicism and prayer.

The Democratic version of the gender gap is actually not much different from Mr. Kristol's, but with a positive spin. Women are voting Democratic, in this view, not because they are emotional and muddle-headed but because they are more compassionate and less aggressive than men, and thus attracted to the party that will help the weakest members of society.

Of course, the view that women are natural liberals—whether that is seen as good or bad—does not explain why more than half of all women voted for Eisenhower, Nixon,

51

and Ronald Reagan. It doesn't explain why so many men support Mr. Clinton today, and it doesn't explain why gender gaps widen and shrink with the times.

So let's dispense with sentimental explanations based on personality or nature. Bellicosity and toughness are by no means a male preserve, nor is compassion a female one. Women, for all their vaunted empathy, have been as willing as men to regard their political and religious enemies as lesser human beings, heathen, or vermin. Affluent women have never shown an especially tender-hearted sympathy toward their sisters in poverty.

Today's gender gap, like the race gap or wealth gap, is primarily caused by issues and economics. As Celinda Lake, a Democratic pollster, found, given a choice between a candidate they agree with on the issues but who has character flaws and a candidate with a good character with whom they disagree, both sexes choose the candidate they agree with, by a large margin.

And that, I think, is what is happening in this election too, except that women are more likely to agree with Bill Clinton than Bob Dole. Polls show that the gender gap emerged and widened as more women than men rejected the philosophy of the Reagan Revolution they once endorsed.

I'd like to think they changed their minds out of compassion, but a more likely motive is experience. A friend told me about a student of hers, an older woman who had returned to college. "I was always against welfare," the woman told my friend. "I thought it coddled the weak. Then my husband divorced me. I was left with nothing. Welfare saved my life until I could get myself together. I learned first-hand how many women are one divorce away from welfare." If a conservative is a liberal man who's been mugged, a liberal is a conservative woman who's been divorced.

The gender gap, then, is largely an experience gap. More women than men today worry that they or their children might need a safety net if they lose a job, lose a partner, or lose their health. More women than men are taking care of aging, infirm parents. Many more single mothers than single fathers are raising children on their own. And young women are learning that sex discrimination in the workplace isn't quite the thing of the past they'd been led to believe.

For women to perceive that Democrats will be more responsive than Republicans to these concerns is neither sentimental nor irrational. It stems from self-interest, surely a motive that conservatives understand. And the many men who share with women concerns about the health of their families, the education of their children, and the stability of their jobs know that these issues are not "feminine," but human.

16
THE PARADOX OF GENDER

Little boys and girls are incredibly "sexist" in their notions of what it means to be a boy or a girl. "A boy can't be a nurse," they will say, or "A girl can't be a doctor." They are typically this stereotyped even when their mothers are doctors. Moreover, boys and girls will often segregate themselves into their own groups for play, even when their parents and teachers try to get them to play together. Why? In the book reviewed in this essay, the author illustrates many guidelines of critical thinking—asking questions, considering the many explanations for children's stereotyped behavior, resisting the tendency to oversimplify (as in "it's all biological" or "it's all learned"), and suggesting that we may have to live with uncertainty about the answers.

Review of *The Two Sexes: Growing Up Apart, Coming Together*
By Eleanor E. Maccoby
Bellnap Press of Harvard University Press, 1998

Scientific American, October 1998

Talking about sex differences is America's second favorite indoor sport. (The first is practicing them.) Women wonder why little boys love guns, dump trucks, and robots, why men hog the remote, and why their husbands don't talk about their feelings. Men wonder why women talk so much about feelings and don't just get on with it. Maybe, we privately think, scientists really will one day discover a techno-gizmo gene on the Y chromosome and a recessive verbo-blather gene on the X.

Everyone is fascinated by sex differences, and that's the problem for researchers who study them. More than any other topic of inquiry, we *live* this one—in our beds, boardrooms, playgrounds, kitchens—so we all have our favorite theories that fit our experiences and prejudices. Scientists, though, must confront what they call "the paradox of gender": the fact that while they are rummaging around in their laboratories trying to find sex differences and locate their origins, in the outside world sex differences rise and fall as rapidly as hemlines and stock prices.

In *The Two Sexes*, Eleanor E. Maccoby, a former professor of psychology at Stanford University and a member of the national Academy of Sciences, has taken a terrific stab at the paradox of gender. The most important theme of her book is that the behavior we attribute to gender is not a matter of individual personality; it is an emergent property of relationships and groups. What people say, what they do, and how they speak with members of their own sex differ considerably from how they behave when the other sex is around. Maccoby shows that gender differences in children couldn't be accounted for by personality traits but rather by the gender composition of a group. Little girls aren't "passive" as some ingrained quality, for example; they are passive only when boys are present.

This approach shows why traditional efforts to measure sex differences in terms of individual traits or abilities (empathy, vanity, submissiveness, intelligence, math abilities, and so forth) are fruitless and become quickly dated. Sex differences that show up in any study tend to be artifacts of education, power, the immediate social context, and the historical moment, which is why they wax and wane with the times. For example, "female intuition" about other people is actually subordinate's intuition: both sexes are equally intuitive when they have to read a superior's mood, nonverbal signals, or intentions, and equally thick-headed, when they are the bosses, about their subordinates' feelings.

Maccoby sets out to explain the great mystery of gender development: the virtually universal existence of gender segregation among children, which remains impervious to the best efforts of egalitarian-minded parents and teachers. Boys and girls will play together if adults require them to, al-though it's often "side-by-side" play, in which each does his or her own thing; but given their druthers, children self-segregate. The result, Maccoby argues, is the emergence of a "girls' culture" and a "boys' culture" that are strikingly different in play styles, toy preferences, and ways of interacting. Before long, as with any two nations, schools, or ethnic groups, boys and girls identify with their own in-group, they stereotype and disparage members of the out-group, and they misunderstand or feel uncomfortable with the other group's ways of doing things.

The most puzzling fact about the two cultures of gender, however, is their symmetry. Boys' groups, Maccoby shows, are "more cohesive than girls' groups: more sexist, more exclusionary, more vigilant about gender-boundary violations by their members, and more separate from adult culture." Throughout childhood, as throughout life, there are fewer penalties for girls who encroach on boys' turf and who like to do boy things than for boys who venture onto girls' territory.

And so the great question is: Why? Why are children, in the words of sociologist John H. Gagnon, the Gender Police, enforcing rigid stereotypes that many of their parents have long discarded? Why do they behave differently with their own sex than with the other? And what, if anything, is the link between childhood and adulthood, considering how many members of the Gender Police eventually become gender criminals, breaking as many gender rules as they can, or gender revolutionaries, trying to rewrite the rules altogether? Maccoby's answers are both timely and old-fashioned, falling squarely between two antithetical trends in the current study of gender.

Opposite or Other?

One, the oldest empirical tradition, takes an essentialist approach. Essentialists regard a gender-related attitude, trait, or behavior as being something embedded in the person—internal, persistent, consistent across situations and time—and thus they tend to regard the sexes as "opposites": men are aggressive, women pacifistic; men are rational, women emotional. The most extreme version of essentialism is represented by pop-psychologist John Gray, who thinks men are from Mars and women are from Venus. But here on Earth all kinds of other notions of inherent sexual opposition are widespread. For Jungians and psychoanalysts, men and women are guided by opposite archetypes and unconscious dynamics. For some feminist psychologists, men and women have inherently different ways of knowing, ways of speaking, ways of moral reasoning, and the like. For neuroscientists, men's and women's brains operate differently. For sociobiologists, male promiscuity and female monogamy are opposite, hard-wired reproductive strategies. (When sociobiologists learned that the males of many species are nurturant and monogamous and the females of most species are promiscuous, they reconnoitered and decided that these reproductive strategies too are adaptive.)

In contrast, researchers who take a social constructionist approach vigorously dispute all forms of essentialism. Social constructionists hold that there is no "essence" of masculinity and femininity, for these concepts and labels are endlessly changing, constructed from the eye of the observer and from the historical and economic conditions of our lives. "Opposition," for example, is a social construction, not an empirical reality; it is a stereotype that blinds us to the greater evidence of gender similarity. Are men rational? Sure, except in love, war, and sporting events. Are women unaggressive? Sure, unless you define "aggressiveness" as the intention to harm another, in which case they don't differ from men; it's just that female aggressiveness often takes a different form—verbal abuse, humiliation, or the exclusion of other females from the group. Constructionists regard gender as a performance, not an attribute. People don't *have* a gender, they *do* gender, which is why their behavior changes so much depending on the situation. A teenage boy may "do" masculine when he's with a pack of his male friends but "do" feminine by tenderly caring for his baby brother (if his friends aren't watching).

For the constructionists, therefore, the really interesting news about gender lies not in the traditional oppositional categories but in the increasingly diverse and growing numbers of people who aren't conforming to the categories at all—even to the fundamental categories of male and female. Biologists such as Anne Fausto-Sterling and others have shown that human dimorphism is neither as obvious nor as universal as most people believe. The number of "intersexed" infants born with anatomical, hormonal, or genotypic ambiguities is about 2 percent of all live births—a small percentage, but one that comprises many thousands of individuals. Books in this genre include Suzanne J. Kessler's *Lessons from the Intersexed*, Marianne van den Wijngaard's *Reinventing the Sexes*, and Alice D. Dreger's *Hermaphrodites and the Medical Invention of Sex*.

Maccoby, calling her book *The Two Sexes*, is not remotely interested in the "transgender" research that is revolutionizing gender studies; she finds the whole subject tangential to the question of male-female differences. Yet she also rejects biological reductionism and other essentialist ideas of opposition. She refers always to the "other" sex, never the "opposite" sex; she never assumes that biology is the whole story, emphasizing repeatedly that it interacts with experience and culture. For example, childhood sex segregation may be universal, but it differs in form and degree depending on culture. Societies in which men clearly have higher status than women, Maccoby reports, are those in which boys make "the earliest and strongest efforts to distance themselves from women and girls—from their own mothers, as well as from other females."

In the second part, Maccoby reviews the voluminous research on biological factors, socialization practices, and cognitive processes that might explain the mystery of children's self-segregation. Many of the findings here are fascinating. For instance, sex segregation does not originate because boys have a greater "activity level," as commonly believed. In fact, boys aren't more physically active than girls when children are playing on their own. But when boys play with other boys, they become more excited and aroused than girls do and by different things: threats, challenges, and competition. High rates of male activity are a *consequence* of male-male play, not a cause. Besides, activity levels decline from ages four to six, when gender segregation steadily increases.

Maccoby, a scrupulous scientist, gives us a state-of-the-art review of the research, not a cohesive argument designed to support a thesis. In this age of simplistic pop-psych overgeneralizations, her caution and scholarly rigor are refreshing. Yet readers may occasionally get lost in the dense thickets of evidence for and against each line of explanation. I felt I was eating many delicious raisins while being denied the satisfaction of a whole piece of cake.

The third section of the book, in which Maccoby examines the links between childhood and adulthood, is the weakest, perhaps because of her own ambivalence. On the one hand, she argues that the gender segregation established in childhood and the asymmetrical cultural differences that result from it persist in many adult contexts, including the workforce and men's and women's habits, preferences, and disputes. Many men don't listen to their wives, Maccoby suggests, for the same reason that little boys refuse to be influenced by little girls.

On the other hand, she subtitles her book "Growing Up Apart, Coming Together," which accurately reflects the fact that vast changes in men's and women's relationships have occurred "in spite of, rather than because of, the way boys and girls are socialized by their parents," and in spite of, I might add, sex differences in hormones or alleged brain function. Among adults, circumstances and experiences supersede the maturational pull of genes and hormones and even the socializing pull of parental instruction. That is why a random group of 50-year-olds is more diverse than a group of five-year-olds and why adults today find themselves doing things they once would never have imagined for themselves. And it's why Maccoby's generalizations about adults seem flat and stereotypic, although certainly they have an element of truth, in contrast to her brilliant portrayal of children.

The war between essentialists and constructionists is bound to continue, and this book will provide ammunition for both sides. But perhaps the war between men and women will find a lasting truce if, as Maccoby hopes, we understand that men and women don't have to be the same in order to be equal in opportunities, income, or love.

17

BIOLOGICAL POLITICS AND THE STUDY OF GENDER

The explosion of biological research has been enormously exciting, as scientists peer into the brain with PET scans and decode the human genome with what seems like astonishing speed. How should critical thinkers think about this biological revolution? How can we accept its contributions without oversimplifying and reducing all of the complexities of behavior to genes, brain cells, and hormones? And when it comes to topics that have political and social implications, such as differences between the sexes or between ethnic groups, why should the public be especially careful about biological findings? This essay suggests some "rules of the road" for thinking critically about biological findings that make the news.

Rules of the Road for Biological Research

The Los Angeles Times

July 19, 1998

My earliest ambition, at age 6, was to be the world's first woman bus driver. Before long, I saw that women were as rare as egrets in bus driving and a whole lot of other occupations, too, including law, medicine, law enforcement, science, news reporting, bartending, real estate, and insurance. That was then.

I got to thinking about the progress and setbacks on the road to sexual equality that I have witnessed in my lifetime as I was reading an article called "The Female Brain." The writer began with the usual caveats: There are more differences within any group of male brains or female brains than there are between the two sexes; moreover, experience and stimulation change the brain throughout life. Then, cheerfully throwing these cautions aside, the writer proceeded to generalize about "the female brain." (Not, you notice, *some* female brains or Louise's brain; "the" female brain.)

My first automatic reaction was to say, "Here we go again." Like most people who support equal rights for women or other stigmatized groups, I am uncomfortable about biological research, with good reason: It has a long and inglorious history of justifying discrimination and bigotry. Yet it will no longer do to take a reflexively anti-biological stance toward every finding that makes the news. It is indisputable that biology plays an important role in intelligence, temperament, emotion, obesity, ulcers, schizophrenia, and many other areas once thought to be purely psychological. Why not sex differences in the brain?

Biological research has long been polarized between the social conservatives who love it and the social reformists who hate it. Conservatives typically welcome biological findings, because such evidence seems to support their belief in the immutability of human nature and group differences. Liberals tend to reject biological findings, because such evidence seems to dispute their hopes for improving the human condition. But in fact both sides often make the same mistake: They assume that if something is "biological," it's permanent and fixed, whereas if it's learned, it can readily be changed.

This clash of assumptions erupted in the heated controversy a few years ago over *The Bell Curve,* by conservatives Charles Murray and Richard Herrnstein. The authors argued that because IQs are largely genetically determined, there's little point spending money on social programs designed to raise the IQs of lower-scoring groups (read: African-Americans). Liberals replied with scathing attacks on the authors' methods and their argument of a genetic contribution to intelligence.

In fact, the pro-biology forces are right that genes do set a range for our intellectual abilities; but the pro-learning forces are also right that experience, stimulation, and nutrition determine where in a given range anyone actually falls. That's why behavior and abilities that have a biological component can indeed be affected by learning. Conversely, some learned behavior can become deeply ingrained and almost impossible to modify. Most people, for example, do not easily change their religious beliefs, sexual attitudes, prejudices— or even their table manners, despite the best efforts of their spouses.

Biological findings don't automatically dictate a conservative social policy; rather, our goals and values determine how we will use biological research (or any other). For example, future evidence of a genetic contribution to homosexuality could be used to promote acceptance of a normal variation in sexual orientation, or to find ways of eradicating this biological "defect." Biology doesn't cause homophobia; homophobia causes a misuse of biology.

We can, I think, accept the contributions of biology as long as we resist the tendency to reduce complex problems and behaviors to a few physiological mechanisms. I propose a few guidelines to help assess biological findings in the news:

• Be wary of first findings; always wait for scientists to replicate the research. Findings from biology somehow seem more solid and reliable than, say, findings on family influences. The brain, after all, is a physical thing; you can touch it, probe it, scan it. In reality, however, there is far more subjectivity in brain and genetics studies than most people realize, and far more variation in physiology. For example, everyone got excited when genes were reported for manic-depression, sensation-seeking, and a kind of alcoholism, respectively. But scientists have so far been unable to reproduce these findings.

• Be wary of anyone who overgeneralizes from small samples or uncertain evidence. Always ask: What, if anything, do these findings mean? In one study that made headlines, 19 men and 19 women had to do a task requiring them to process and compare sounds. MRI scans showed that in both sexes, an area at the front of the left hemisphere was activated. But in 11 women and none of the men, the corresponding area in the right hemisphere was also active. This result supports the idea that male brains are more specialized for some functions.

This study was used to explain everything from why men won't ask for directions to why women have greater intuition (which, by the way, studies show is actually "subordinate's" intuition and hardly unique to women). What everyone seemed to miss was that there was no difference whatever in how men and women actually performed on the task. What, then, are the real-life implications of this study? Maybe none. Or maybe it explains why left-hemisphere damage is less likely to cause language problems in women than in men after a stroke, or why some women compensate better than men do for reading disabilities. But at this point, no one knows; it's all speculation.

• Remember that an average difference between groups always involves enormous overlap between them; when we focus on the differences, we forget the greater similarities. If there are average differences between male and female brains in some respect, that would no more mean there is a generic "female brain" or "male brain" than there is a Japanese brain or even a politician's brain.

• Finally, if repeated studies reliably find biological contributions to a meaningful sex difference, then our job is to make sure these findings are used intelligently. Suppose there is a genetic or hormonal reason that boys, on the average, are more likely than girls to have reading disabilities and do better on spatial reasoning tests. This news could be used stupidly, for example by sexists who overlook the fact that most boys and girls are alike in math and reading and who want to justify their belief that females don't belong in science. But the news could also be used wisely, if it led to new ways of helping more boys learn to read better and more girls succeed in math.

Now it's time for a pop quiz: What is the connection between research on "the female brain" and the worldwide upheaval in women's roles, sexual behavior, and status?

That's right: Nothing. The revolution in gender rules and roles has occurred because of changes in technology, birth control, the economy, and worldwide modernization, not because of genes, hormones, or left-brain/right-brain differences. If there are sex differences in the brain, they have nothing to do with struggles over fair pay, economic security, and who does the dishes. Sexual equality is not hard-wired; it is hard won.

PART IV

APPLYING PSYCHOLOGY
TO SOCIAL ISSUES

18

EMOTIONAL EPIDEMICS AND THEIR CONSEQUENCES

Where do our attitudes and beliefs come from? Why do some people come to believe they were abducted by aliens, have 354 personalities, or were victimized by satanic ritual abuse cults that forced them to eat babies? Critical thinkers resist easy answers (such as "those folks are plain crazy" or "if they say it happened to them, it must be true") and look instead at the larger social and cultural influences on people's beliefs—including the power of the media to promote certain narrative explanations of mysterious phenomena that lack obvious answers. As the book reviewed here shows, "hysterical epidemics" and emotional "contagions" are normal social phenomena, but it's not always easy to tell when we are in the midst of one.

Review of *Hystories: Hysterical Epidemics and Modern Media*
By Elaine Showalter
Columbia University Press, 1997

The New York Times Book Review,
May 4, 1997

The theories of Sigmund Freud are the crabgrass in the lawn of cultural criticism. Scientists, philosophers, and research psychologists have been trying for decades to dynamite the tenacious stuff, poison it, or pull it up by its roots, but it keeps coming back. The plump and juicy metaphors of Freudian analysis are just too appealing to many literary critics, because they account nicely for any topic under scrutiny—on a *post hoc* basis, that is. The fact that three Freudians will analyze the same person or phenomenon in three different ways never fazes Freud's supporters, any more than does the fact that three movie critics will review the same movie in three different ways. But that is precisely why Freudian metaphors appeal to literary critics and exasperate scientists, and why this book will do the same.

Elaine Showalter, a professor of English and president-elect of the Modern Language Association, has written a spirited Freudo-literary analysis of what she calls hysterical epidemics and what social scientists call "emotional contagions" or mass psychogenic illnesses. Her six examples are chronic fatigue syndrome,

Gulf War syndrome, recovered memories of sexual abuse, multiple personality disorder, satanic ritual abuse, and alien abduction. She knows full well that throwing the first three into the mix will "infuriate thousands of people who believe they are suffering from unidentified organic disorders or the after-effects of trauma." She braves not only their wrath, but also that of the feminist therapists and writers whose "credulous endorsements of recovered memory and satanic abuse" have contributed to these epidemics. This attitude alone is worth the price of the book.

It may seem odd and unduly provocative that a scholar who has written about misogynistic attitudes in medicine would retain the word "hysteria," laden as it is with muddled meanings and antiwoman baggage. But Showalter wants to reclaim "hysteria" as a universal human response to conflict, anxiety, or sexual desire. When these strong feelings cannot be expressed directly, she argues, they are transformed into a vast and shifting array of physical symptoms or delusional beliefs. Hysteria is a culturally permissible language of distress, used by those who are otherwise mute or silenced. A man who cannot admit he is afraid can legitimately complain of having a headache; a woman who is afraid to acknowledge her sexual fantasies can legitimately claim she was abducted by aliens who subjected her to "probes."

Hysteria becomes epidemic, Showalter maintains, through the spread of culturally fashionable narratives, which she calls "hystories." A hystory is picked up by the news media, talk shows, self-help books, and the Internet; named and validated by medical or psychological experts; and given a congenial reception by society. "Multiple personality disorder," for example, was sparked by the media's obsession with sensational cases, like that of Sybil; endorsed by psychiatrists, who then went looking for it in their patients; perpetuated by the growth of professional groups, journals, and treatment centers devoted to it; and welcomed by feminists who saw it as the ultimate consequence of women's victimization and loss of self.

Some aspects of these epidemics do lend themselves beautifully to literary study. For example, Showalter traces the similarity between popular forms of women's pornography, such as the "soft-core rape fantasies of bodice busters," and the erotic scenarios of women who say they have been abducted by aliens. And she shows that when therapists and doctors express surprise that their patients independently tell the same story—of what an alien looks like, of "memories" of a ritual massacre of babies and goats—they are failing to recognize how common these "plot lines" are in our culture.

The "hysterical narrative," Showalter tells us, has become a growth industry in literary criticism, emerging "at the busy crossroad where psychoanalytic theory, narratology, feminist criticism and the history of medicine intersect." Normally I would think it unfair to fault her for staying in the ethereal territory she

64

knows and not moving on down the road. But the Freudo-literary tradition is not just an intellectual exercise for the flexing of academic muscles; it has had powerful and pernicious effects on people's lives. Indeed, discredited Freudian theories and invalidated methods, along with the widespread ignorance of the difference between scientific research and clinical/literary opinion, have contributed to three of the very epidemics she discusses: recovered memory, multiple personality, and satanic ritual abuse. This is why Showalter's approach, while often informative, suffers from three fundamental flaws.

The first is that it loses its grounding in the circumstances and realities of people's lives. Sometimes a headache is a "language of distress," and sometimes it's a tumor. Because Showalter sees hystories as an unwitting collusion between troubled victims and sympathetic experts who offer a clear reason for the patient's unhappiness (it's all due to your dad, the aliens, a yet-unnamed disease, a government conspiracy), she allocates no blame to either side. "Hystories are constructed," she writes, "by suffering, caring psychologists, dedicated clergy, devoted parents, hardworking police, concerned feminists and anxious communities."

Indeed, but such narratives are also constructed by vested interests protecting their professions and incomes, ignorant psychologists, greedy opportunists who see a way to make a fast buck on the insecurities of the vulnerable, ideologues of the right and left, and clergy and politicians drunk on the elixir of moral righteousness. By not also identifying the venal motives that support the epidemics, let alone their economic, social, and political supports, Showalter implies that they are merely psychological phenomena, reflecting people's efforts in scary times to reduce anxiety. So they are; but they are also big business.

Second, while Showalter correctly alerts us to the medicalizing of problems caused by strong emotions and psychological stresses, she overlooks an equally common diagnostic error: the psychologizing of problems with organic causes. Until the bacillus that causes tuberculosis was identified, TB was thought to be a result of having a "tubercular personality." Until the bacterium that causes peptic ulcers was identified, ulcers were said to be caused by repressed anger, which is still a favorite psychoanalytic culprit. In California, a woman spent 12 years in therapy, her muscles getting steadily weaker until she couldn't lift her hand to brush her teeth. The psychiatrist said that her problem was her "repressed rage" at her parents; she turned out to have myasthenia gravis, a progressive muscular disease.

In this context, Showalter's discussion of Gulf War syndrome is both informative and limited. "War makes people sick," she says succinctly. The sickness has had different names— shell shock, war neurosis, post-traumatic stress disorder—and taken different forms, but it is caused by the terror, stress, and unpredictability of battle. After World War I, she writes, men across Europe complained of "limps, loss of voice, paralyzed limbs, headaches, amnesia, incapacitating insomnia and emotional distress." An English military doctor, not wanting to accuse British soldiers of being "hysterical" (i.e., weak and womanly), suggested that the symptoms were caused by the physical or chemical effects of exposure to an exploding shell; hence the term shell shock. Today, as then, Showalter argues, veterans are hostile to the idea that any aspect of their suffering might be psychological.

By tracing the similarity of veterans' various symptoms—so vague, so diverse—across time, Showalter makes a convincing argument that emotional contagion and panic are a big part of Gulf War syndrome. For example, some veterans attribute their babies' respiratory problems to the syndrome, but studies find the rate of these infants' problems to be no higher than usual.

Yet it is not irrational or hysterical for veterans to believe that they might have been exposed to chemical toxins in the Gulf War and that the Government has been lying to them. Government agencies do not have a sterling record of voluntarily revealing their deadly blunders. *[NOTE: In late 1999, a small study found evidence suggesting that some soldiers with "Gulf War syndrome" have brain abnormalities that might have resulted from chemicals they were exposed to during the war.]* Similarly, although many of the people who claim to have chronic fatigue syndrome are probably suffering from depression and other normal maladies

of modern life, it is unlikely that all of them are. In the absence of medical certainty, the belief that *all* such symptoms are psychological in origin is no improvement over the belief that none of them are.

Finally, the deepest flaw in this book stems from her confusion about the difference between the empirical tradition of psychology and the literary one of Freudianism, and her persistent mistaken equation of psychotherapy with psychoanalysis. She acknowledges the devastating new criticism of Freud and his work, agreeing that he pressured his patients "to produce narratives congruent with his theories," thereby eliciting "confabulations rather than actual memories"; and that his treatment of Dora, the classical case of hysteria, was bullying and unethical. But then, in a dazzling non sequitur, she attacks the critics who made the word aware of Freud's failings as "anti-Freudian zealots," concluding that "whatever the assaults of academics and renegades, artists and writers will continue to cherish Freudian insights." This is like saying, "Whatever the evidence of biologists and physicians, artists and writers will continue to think that repressed anger causes ulcers."

The Freudian-literary alliance thus perpetuates a fuzzy-headed antipathy to evidence and logic in the name of post-modern relativism and "narrative analysis" : If all stories are equally therapeutic and valid from the storyteller's point of view, who am I to judge them? That is the attitude that contributes most to the spread of hysterical epidemics. "I have no idea if my client was really subjected to satanic ritual abuse," one therapist told her colleagues at a conference. "My job is to believe her." This remark is plain nonsense. Therapists don't have to believe their clients, or believe that there is only one truth, in order to teach their clients to think critically about their lives, to look for the evidence for their beliefs, and to examine many reasons for their unhappiness.

Ironically, Showalter makes a vigorous case that not all narratives are equally therapeutic or true, that we must rely on clear thinking and evidence to protect us from the lure of emotional contagions and irrational beliefs. For all the problems I had with the specifics of her argument, therefore, I am grateful for her resounding call to arms against the witch hunts, delusions, and follies of our times.

19

THE DAY-CARE SEX-ABUSE SCANDALS

No topic evokes more emotion, and emotional reasoning, than the abuse of children—particularly the sexual abuse of children. What happens when good intentions, such as the desire to protect children and prosecute offenders, get out of hand precisely because of that emotional reasoning? And when good intentions go too far, resulting in the incarceration of people falsely accused of abuse, what prevents their accusers from saying, "I was wrong"? Can solid psychological research on children's testimony and mental development help us make better decisions in individual cases where sexual abuse is alleged to have occurred?

A Day-Care Witch Hunt Tests Justice in Massachusetts

The Los Angeles Times

April 11, 1997

A few weeks ago, Massachusetts' Supreme Judicial Court reinstated the convictions of Gerald Amirault, 42, his sister Cheryl Amirault LeFave, 38, and their mother Violet Amirault, 73, all found guilty and sent to prison in 1986-87 for molesting children at their day-care center.

Except for the names and the outcome, the Amirault story is identical to that of the McMartins, whose trial devastated Los Angeles in the late 1980s, and the Little Rascals day-care case in North Carolina, the Kelly Michaels case in New Jersey, Dale Akiki's in San Diego, and to the alleged molestation rings in Jordan, Minn.; Wenatchee, Wash.; Niles,

Mich., and dozens of other communities across America.

These cases made headlines, made careers, and destroyed lives. One by one, they crumbled in court or were overturned on appeal; but not in the state of Salem. The Massachusetts high court rejected the Amiraults' contention that their trial was constitutionally flawed by a special courtroom seating arrangement that had denied them the ability to look the child witnesses in the eye. In a 6-1 ruling, the justices allowed that some of the charges made against the Amiraults by the children were "quite improbable" and may have resulted from "communicated hysteria," but the public deserves a sense of "finality" in criminal cases. "The mere fact that, if the process were redone, there might be a different outcome, or that some lingering doubt about the first outcome may remain, cannot be a sufficient reason to reopen what society has a right to consider closed," the court said. In other words, justice is less important than closure.

I have a personal interest in the fate of the Amiraults, because I am still trying to atone for an essay I wrote about the McMartin case for *The Los Angeles Times* years ago. When the trial ended in a hung jury, several jurors said they had been dismayed (and thank God, unpersuaded) by the coercive interviewing tactics of prosecution witness Kee MacFarlane, a social worker who had been called on to determine whether the children had been molested. I hadn't read MacFarlane's testimony, but I thought I understood her approach. At the time, research suggested that children often will not tell about an uncomfortable or shameful experience unless the interviewer asks leading questions (such as "The doctor touched your private parts, didn't he?"). So that's what I wrote in my essay, which was titled by the editors, "Do Children Lie? Not About This."

Since then, of course, it has become abundantly clear not only that children do lie, on occasion, but also that they can be influenced to make false allegations, just as adults can. Today behavioral scientists who study children's testimony recognize that framing the issue in terms of "children never lie" versus "children always lie" is wrong. Instead, they ask: Under what conditions is a child more likely to be suggestible and claim that something happened that did not? Here are some answers:

• When the child is very young, under 3 or 4.
• When the situation is emotionally intense.
• When interviewers encourage the blurring of fantasy and reality, for instance by asking the child to "pretend" that an adult did something to them.
• When the child has a desire to please an interviewer.
• When an adult repeatedly asks the same question; many children (especially preschoolers) will then change their answers, thinking the first one was wrong or unacceptable.
• When the child is pressured by threats, offered bribes, or accused of lying if they don't give the "right" answers.
• When the child is asked to play with anatomically detailed dolls. The assumption has been that doll play will reveal abuse that the child is ashamed to admit. However, when researchers compare how abused and nonabused children play with the dolls, they find no differences. Even nonabused children play with the dolls in a sexual manner; those parts are pretty interesting! With preschoolers, the use of dolls may even increase memory errors and erroneous reports of sexual touch.

All of these mistakes were present in the interrogations of children in every one of the sensational cases of the 1980s. In addition, there was no way the children or defendants could convince the prosecutors that molestation had not occurred. If the children admitted it after hours of questioning, that was evidence; but if they denied it, that too was evidence—evidence that they were too scared, or in denial, or had repressed the memory.

A study by Sena Garven shows how alarmingly easy it is to get young children to agree to false allegations against an adult. A young man visited 3- to 6-year-old children in their preschool, read a story, and handed out treats. A week later, Garven questioned them about his visit. She asked children in one group leading questions to see how many false allegations the children would agree with: Did he shove the teacher? Did he steal a pencil from the teacher's desk? Did he throw a crayon at a kid who was talking?

Then Garven asked children in another group the same questions, but she added techniques used in the McMartin, Kelly Michaels, and Amirault trials: telling the children what "other kids" had supposedly said; asking the children to "help"; expressing disappointment if answers were negative, and praising the child for making allegations that the adult wanted to hear.

In the first group, children affirmed about 15 percent of the false allegations of wrongdoing—bad enough for those who think that children never lie, misremember, or make things up. But in the second group, the 3-year-olds said "yes" to about 75 percent of false allegations offered to them, and about 50 percent of the 4- to-6-year-olds did the same. And this was with a short interview, lasting only five to ten minutes. In the major day-care abuse trials, the interviewers kept up their questioning over the course of many weeks.

Research like this has helped psychologists understand how children can best be interviewed to increase the accuracy of what they tell. It has helped to free falsely accused people from prison. It has demonstrated the necessity of videotaping all interviews with children, so that impartial observers can assess potential interviewer bias or coercion.

And yet many children's advocates remain committed to the belief that "children never lie," and that anyone who suggests that children can be induced to tell falsehoods is abetting molesters. I once was sympathetic to their worry that the country will return to the bad old days when no one believed a word a child said. But now that seems more likely an excuse to avoid saying the three hardest words in the English language: "I was wrong."

If we are to learn anything from the Amirault case and its many clones, it is that we must be prepared to change our minds when the evidence dictates. Contrary to the ruling of Massachusetts' Supreme Judicial Court, "closure" never takes a precedence over justice. And there will be no closure on the sorry decade of day-care hysteria on America as long as the Amiraults are in prison.

How Child Witnesses Are Shaped: Cleverly

In New Jersey, Margaret Kelly Michaels was convicted in 1988 of

115 counts of sexual misconduct with 20 preschoolers. Michaels was accused, among other things, of licking peanut butter off children's genitals, making the children drink her urine and eat her feces, and raping the children with knives, forks, and toys. These shocking acts were said to have occurred during school hours over a period of seven months, although no adult had noticed them, no child had complained, and none of the parents had noticed any symptoms or problems in their children.

Michaels was sentenced to 47 years in prison. After serving five years, she was released when an appeals court ruled that she had not received a fair trial because of the way the children were interrogated; the district attorney declined to retry her.

Here are some excerpts from a typical interview of one of the children, reported by Stephen Ceci and Maggie Bruck in *Jeopardy in the Courtroom* (American Psychological Association, 1995):

Social worker: Don't be so unfriendly. I thought we were buddies last time.

Child: Nope, not any more.

Social worker: We have gotten a lot of other kids to help us since I last saw you. . . . Did we tell you that Kelly is in jail?

Child: Yes, my mother already told me.

Social worker: Did I tell you that this [the detective] is the guy that arrested her? . . . Well, we can get out of here quick if you just tell me what you told me the last time, when we met.

Child: I forgot.

Social worker: No, you didn't. I know you didn't.

Child: I did! I did! . . .

Social worker: Oh, come on. We talked to a few more of your buddies. And everyone told me about the nap room, and the bathroom stuff, and the music room stuff, and the choir stuff, and the peanut butter stuff, and everything. . . . All your buddies [talked] . . . Come on, do you want to help us out? Do you want to keep her in jail? I'll let you hear your voice and play with the tape recorder. . . . Real quick, will you just tell me what happened with the wooden spoon? Let's go.

Child: I forgot.

Detective: Now listen, you have to behave.

Social worker: Do you want me to tell him to behave? Are you going to be a good boy, huh? While you were here, did [the detective] show you his badge and his handcuffs? . . . Back to what happened to you with the spoon. If you don't remember words, maybe you can show me [with dolls].

In Massachusetts, the Amirault family was not as lucky as Kelly Michaels. At their trial in 1986, some of their preschool's children said they had been attacked by a robot, forced to eat a frog, or were molested by clowns and lobsters. One boy said he had been tied naked to a tree in the schoolyard in front of all the teachers and children, although all the teachers denied it and no other child verified it. Here is an excerpt from interviews of some of the child witnesses by a pediatric nurse who sometimes used Bert and Ernie puppets to "aid" the children's recall (from *Victims of Memory*, by Mark Pendergrast, Upper Access Press, 1996):

> *Nurse:* Would you tell Ernie?
> *Child:* No.
> *Nurse:* Ah, come on [pleading tone]. Please tell Ernie. Please tell me. Please tell me. So we could help you. Please, . . . you whisper it to Ernie. . . . Did anybody ever touch you right there [pointing to the vagina of a girl doll]?
> *Child:* No.
> *Nurse:* [pointing to the doll's posterior] Did anybody touch your bum?
> *Child:* No.
> *Nurse:* Would you like to tell Bert?
> *Child:* They didn't touch me!
> *Nurse:* Who didn't touch you?
> *Child:* Not my teacher, nobody.

[NOTE: In 1997, awaiting the appeal of their case, Violet Amirault died of cancer. Her son Gerald was permitted to visit her, as she lay dying, for 15 minutes. In 1998, Judge Isaac Borenstein of the Massachusetts Superior Court ruled that Cheryl Amirault LeFave was entitled to a new trial, because of the "weak evidence" that had been used to convict her. "This weak evidence, in combination with and reinforced by constitutional errors and questionable evidence, together with the strength of the newly discovered evidence, casts very serious doubt on the result of this trial," he wrote. "On the whole, I am left with the utmost conviction that all these errors and issues have resulted in a substantial miscarriage of justice."

Judge Borenstein's ruling was appealed once again to the Supreme Judicial Court, which once again ruled on behalf of the prosecutors. But after considerable protest from LeFave's supporters, in October, 1999, the District Attorney agreed to reduce Cheryl's sentence to the years she had already served in prison. Today she is free, but she may not work with children, she may not be alone with any child under the age of 16, and she may not speak about her case in public or to the media. Gerald remains in prison.]

20
THE DEATH PENALTY

Psychology is helping us to understand the many and varied origins of violent behavior. If we learn that a violent adult was physically abused and possibly brain damaged in childhood, does that mean the person should be absolved of responsibility for committing murder? What is the appropriate penalty for such an individual—death, life in prison, psychiatric treatment or other forms of rehabilitation? What if rehabilitation is impossible and there is (yet) no treatment? This essay, written after the murderer Robert Alton Harris was executed in the gas chamber in California, examines the either/or thinking that often clouds this issue.

Passion's Posse Claims a Victim

The Los Angeles Times

April 22, 1992

W "hat reason weaves," wrote Alexander Pope, "by passion is undone." I did not expect Robert Alton Harris's life to be spared; I also did not expect the revulsion I felt when I awoke to the news that, minutes before, he had been executed. What a barbaric nation we are, I thought. In one state we imprison people for life who are caught with a few ounces of marijuana; in another, we let a murderer off with a few years if he killed "only" one person; and across the country we randomly and unevenly impose the ultimate penalty in spasms of self-righteousness.

My despairing thoughts were interrupted by Robert Morgan on KMPC radio, gloating that the "pony-tail-wearing guys from the ACLU" had been defeated, that justice had been done. Laughing, he repeatedly played the old Alka-Selzer ditty ("Plop, plop, fizz, fizz, oh what a relief it is. . .").

For many people, it is indeed a relief that Harris is dead. We need to understand why it is. A passion for justice is the basis of all legal and social systems, but legal and social systems must not be governed by passion. I am grateful that the judicial system doesn't rest on my momentary revenge fantasies, for example. When I am outraged by news of heinous crimes, I want to castrate rapists, hang child molesters upside down in trees, throw bank embezzlers to the mob whose life savings they stole, and cut off the hands of punks who knock down old people and steal their wallets. Fortunately, the justice system restrains me and others who would act, posse-style, in the heat of passion.

The emotions generated by questions of crime and punishment tend to be shaped by opposing ideologies, both of which are guilty of fallacious either/or thinking: Either you're for the victim or you're for the criminal. The conservative right tends to construct the matter this way: "Because I have sympathy for the victim, then I cannot have sympathy for the murderer or be concerned in any way with the forces in biology, upbringing, or society that created him." The liberal left seems to say: "Because I have sympathy for a person whom I believe to be the product of a disturbed biology, upbringing, or society, I am obliged to understand and forgive his behavior, for which he is not responsible."

Both of these positions confound two independent issues: understanding behavior and excusing it. The language of understanding, both in psychology and in law, has been woven into issues of diminished responsibility, which can be used to argue for reduced sentences, if not outright acquittal. We're hearing more and more of these excuses these days. In Texas, Ronnie Shelton pleaded not guilty to 28 counts of rape because, he claimed, he suffered from having excessive testosterone. He was convicted, but every day there seems to be another biological or psychological condition served up as a mitigating factor in murder cases: pre- and post-partum depressions, childhood abuse, adult abuse, trauma, delayed trauma, and the like.

Consider this evidence. A team of researchers compared two groups of imprisoned delinquent teenagers: violent boys (who had committed serious assaults, rape, or murder) and less violent boys (who had taken part in fist-fights, threatened others with weapons, and so on). The researchers discovered among the former a much higher incidence of symptoms associated with temporal lobe seizures, neurological impairment such as blackouts and stumbling, and paranoid thinking. Nearly all of the violent boys (98.6 percent) had at least one neurological abnormality and many had more than one, compared to "only" 66.7 percent of the less violent boys. More than 75 percent of the violent boys, compared to one-third of the others, had suffered head injuries as children, had had serious medical problems, and had been beaten savagely by their parents. Many had endured abuse severe enough to have damaged their central nervous systems.

The attitude of many people is: Who cares what makes these kids aggressive? If they turn out to be criminals, violent, impulsive, and lacking any human compassion and empathy themselves, then they forfeit ours. Put them away. Kill them.

It's an understandable reaction. People are right to demand reliable protection from human beings who lack a moral sense, who lack empathy and connection to others, who can kill as easily as smile—whether the reason for their heartlessness is brain damage, bad parenting, or a psychopathic soul. Support for the death penalty is especially understandable when one learns that Robert Harris once beat a man to death and served only 2 1/2 years in prison.

But, understandable as the "kill 'em" reaction is, it does not serve society's interests. It is not "liberal," but rational and civilized to acknowledge the biological, psychological, and social causes of violence, for every humane society recognizes that some individuals are not responsible for their actions. And it is not "conservative," but rational and self-preserving to demand that society protect us from violent individuals who are not responsible for their actions. If we don't even try to draw such distinctions, we become focused on punishment and learn nothing about prevention.

It is time to get past either/or ideologies. We must *both* protect ourselves and recognize that some individuals cannot control their violent impulses. We can feel heartsick both for victims and for criminals who are physically and mentally impaired. We can allocate resources both to protecting society from murderers and to seeing to it that society produces fewer of them.

Finally, in calm moments when our passions are not being swayed by demagogues and news of horrid crimes, we can think about the children all around us whose brains are being damaged by abuse and neglect. Should we do nothing, and wait until too many of them grow up to be killers? And what will we do with them then? Kill them?

21
THE WAR ON DRUGS

Why has the "war on drugs" been so spectacularly unsuccessful? As this essay explains, psychological research provides some answers, and reveals why "just say no" policies actually ensure that many people will say "yes" to harmful drugs and drug abuse. The next time someone inquires whether you are "for" or "against" the use of psychoactive drugs, consider whether that is really the right question to be asking. What would be a better one? If you were Drug Czar, what drugs, if any, would you want to make illegal, and what programs would you institute to reduce drug abuse?

Drop the Iron Fist and Try Rules of Moderation

The Los Angeles Times

March 19, 1990

Faced with the complexities of drug use, many people are tempted by simple formulas: Don't try to distinguish moderation from abuse; settle only for zero tolerance. Don't separate illegal drugs that are beneficial from those that can be deadly; forbid them all. Don't let the kids have an ounce of wine; it will make them alcoholics. Just say no.

The most ironic consequence of these efforts to eradicate illegal drugs is that they actually increase the chances of drug abuse. There are two reasons for this: Policies of abstinence do not teach young people how to use drugs in moderation; and by focusing on the drugs themselves, such policies ignore the reasons that people use them.

For individuals and for society, policies of abstinence are mistakenly thought to be the best defense against abuse. In fact, the opposite is true. Lower rates of alcohol and drug use have been associated with approaches that emphasize moderation and education, approaches in which young people learn responsible use of alcohol and other social drugs in controlled settings, with less potent forms of a drug, and with information about the hazards of excess.

Cultures in which people drink moderately with their meals—and where children, in the presence of their parents, learn the social rules of drinking—have much lower rates of alcoholism than those in which drinking occurs in bars, in binges, or mostly alone. Study after study has found that alcoholism is much more prevalent in societies that forbid children to drink but regard adult drunkenness with amused tolerance or as a sign of masculinity (such as Ireland and the United States) than in cultures that teach children how to drink responsi-

76

bly but frown on adult drunkenness (such as Italy and Greece). With other drugs too, moderate use—such as the Peruvian Indian custom of chewing coca leaves, or the occasional use of marijuana for social and medical purposes—does not lead to addiction or social problems.

The same pattern holds for other drugs. Throughout history there have been "wars" against opium, cocaine, marijuana, tobacco, and coffee. All that these wars accomplished was to boost the popularity of the drug in question. They stimulate curiosity on the part of people who would not otherwise be interested, and they encourage drug taking for negative purposes, such as to act out anger and resentment of authority.

When a person tries any drug without knowing the rules for its use, he or she typically uses it stupidly, the way many teenagers and college students binge on liquor, for instance. Prohibition was supposed to keep adolescents free from liquor's contaminating influence, a rationale of today's drug policies. Sociologist Joan McCord has documented how that rationale backfired: Males who were teenagers during Prohibition were later more likely to be problem drinkers and to commit many more crimes than men who were adults during that time. The former, never having learned how to drink, overdid it when given the opportunity later on.

An individual's responses to a drug depend on his or her mental set: expectations of what the drug will do and on what he or she wants it to do. Studies have shown that there is noth-ing intrinsic in alcohol or crack that makes consumers violent; but violent, angry, frustrated individuals tend to be drawn to these drugs. Similarly, people's responses to drugs depend on the physical and social setting in which the drugs are used. A century ago in this country, marijuana was used as a mild sedative, and cocaine was widely touted as a cure for everything from toothaches to timidity. When cultural outsiders began using these drugs for mind-altering purposes, society responded by making the drugs illegal. That was the first step toward making them major social problems.

When an approach to a problem is repeatedly tried and repeatedly fails, surely it is time to try something else. The alternative to prohibition and enforcement is not legalizing drugs and crossing our fingers. It is drug education, training in the moderate use of some drugs, and continued social sanctions against abuse.

What would such a program of legalization and education look like? The answers are already apparent in the case of cigarettes. Cigarette smoking has significantly declined because of a combination of factors: limits on advertising; rapidly changing attitudes about smoking; and regulations restricting when and where people may smoke. As is the case with tobacco, legalizing marijuana, cocaine, and heroin would not signify an endorsement of their use. Society could continue to prohibit drug abuse on the job, drug advertising, and the use of drugs while driving, operating machinery, or in certain public settings.

But most important, as physician Andrew Weil observed years ago, legalizing drugs must be accompanied by real drug education on a widespread basis. "What passes for education today," he said, is "a thinly disguised attempt to scare people away from the drugs we don't like by exaggerating their dangers." A more truthful program must avoid this hypocrisy. Children would learn that not all drugs are equally hazardous and that some illegal drugs are safer than legal ones. For example, marijuana has some important medical properties. It lessens pain, lessens the nausea that often accompanies chemotherapy, and reduces the swelling in glaucoma, whereas tobacco poses unacceptably high health risks. Children would learn about the dangers of alcohol as well as the dangers of crack, and they would learn the positive reasons for moderate use, such as relaxation, meditation, and socializing.

Education would also emphasize the risks of what Weil calls "problem sets" (consuming drugs to alter bad moods or escape boredom) and "problem settings" (in which people abuse drugs as a condition of membership or way of life). Lessons about moderation and self-control will depend on the reason a person drinks or uses drugs in the first place: In order to pass for 21 in a bar? To join a fraternity or gang? To escape illiteracy or hopelessness? To quiet the despair of a dead-end life?

Many people worry that legalizing drugs will mean that everyone will choose to be high all the time. Perhaps some would for a while, just as dieters sometimes binge on chocolate and involuntary teetotalers binged on drink after Prohibition. And perhaps some people, like the sad lost youths who inhabit the legal-drug parks of Europe, would give over their lives to pursuit of the constant high. There are costs to any policy decisions we make. But the evidence suggests that there will be fewer human, economic, and social costs to a policy of legalization-and-education than to continued escalation of an unwinnable war.

22

ADOLESCENT VIOLENCE

This column was written a year before the shooting rampage at Columbine High School in Littleton, Colorado, which itself followed a series of shocking events in which young boys and teenage males shot and killed their classmates and sometimes adults. Appalling though these events are, however, it is important to keep the larger picture in mind: that teenage violence all over the United States has actually decreased significantly. What do you think are the primary reasons that these individual boys committed such shocking acts of violence? Why is it always males, and never females, who are the killers? Do you think that anything can be done to prevent these random and unpredictable eruptions, or are they, by definition, rare tragedies that are an inescapable part of modern life? For example, do you favor "zero tolerance" policies—such as "crackdowns" on teenagers in high schools, metal detectors in schools, expulsions for even minor infractions of the rules, and locker searches—or do you think such policies unfairly abridge the freedoms of the peaceful and law-abiding majority?

Violence Is a Symptom, Not an Inevitability

The Los Angeles Times

May 24, 1998

Oh no, we say, reading the news with horror and helplessness, another teenage boy on a murderous rampage. This time it's a 15-year-old in Oregon who killed his parents and two fellow students. We haven't recovered from the 11- and 13- year-olds in Jonesboro, Ark., who killed a teacher and four students on March 24.

These acts of vengeful cruelty, occurring not in the mean, bad, big city but in close-knit small communities, are especially threatening to our sense of safety and order. But before we leap to simplistic solutions—build more prisons! Extend the death penalty to 11-year-olds!—let's think about what these murders tell us.

First, they are the aberrations of disturbed individuals, not necessarily a sign that society is falling apart. On the contrary, rates of violence have plummeted in recent years, and nowhere more noticeably than in New York and Los Angeles. When I moved back to Los Angeles in the 1980s, deaths caused by gang warfare were constantly in the news. The sharp decline in gang-related killings has been one of the most remarkable events in this city's recent history.

Second, consider the locations of the last seven school killings in the

United States: Pearl, Mississippi; West Paducah, Kentucky; Stamps, Arkansas; Jonesboro, Arkansas; Edinboro, Pennsylvania; Fayetteville, Tennessee; and Springfield, Oregon. All of these states promote the use of guns for hunting and "protection," and foster what social psychologist Richard Nisbett calls a "culture of honor" that teaches its males to avenge perceived slights and insults. The boys who committed these murders had been taught to use and value guns all their young lives.

Third, all of the perpetrators are male. Psychologists have identified a major divergence in the way boys and girls handle emotional problems, starting in early adolescence: In general, girls begin to internalize anger, anxiety, or low self-esteem by developing eating disorders or depression; boys externalize these problems by drinking too much alcohol or attacking others.

Fourth, from what has been reported thus far, the psychology, history, and motives of the perpetrators differ, which is why efforts to find a single explanation for their actions are likely to fail. Kipland Kinkel, the Oregon teenager, apparently had some of the classic symptoms of anti-social personality disorder or even schizophrenia; he resisted his parents' efforts to discipline him and later said he "heard voices" in his head. But one of the two boys in Jonesboro may have suffered no more than normal adolescent misery and the other normal vulnerability to a more dominant peer.

By understanding the similarities and differences across these horrible acts of murder, we can focus on the diversity of solutions necessary to prevent further ones. Gun control is at the top of my list.

However, there are other interventions to be made. Boys (and girls) need to learn that loneliness, despair, anger, and insecurity will always be part of the human condition, but that there are ways to cope other than by the destruction of oneself or others. They need skills to counter the lessons of the media, which may be summarized as "Mad at someone? Just blow the guy away." Some schools across the country have developed anger-management classes that teach kids constructive alternatives to acting out. Further, parents and teachers need help in recognizing the symptoms of depression and potentially lethal aggression, especially in boys, so that they will not dismiss these symptoms as normal boyishness.

But I fear that the tendency on the part of adults will be to try to crack down on all teenagers by instituting harsh policies of "zero tolerance" that abridge the freedoms of the law-abiding majority, in order to try to prevent any possible incident of future violence. Such a goal is as unreasonable in protecting teenagers as it would be in protecting the rest of us from the lonely, depressed adult men who occasionally go on a rampage and kill their families and co-workers. The price of living in a culture of honor, one that values having free and easy access to guns and ammunition as a basic human right, is that crazy, random acts of violence will continue.

Cultures of honor are hard to change, but even here we can be hopeful. Cultures change when the need for violence within them diminishes. The Vikings were once the most aggressive and barbarous of men; today, you don't hear about squadrons of marauding Scandinavians. But we needn't look to other nations or centuries to see improvements; we can look to the progress of gangs right here in Los Angeles. The lesson they teach us is that violence is a symptom, not an inevitability.

23
BYSTANDER APATHY

Some of the most disturbing stories in the news are about crowds of people who see someone being hurt or even killed and who do nothing. "What's wrong with those people?" we may ask. But as this article shows, the fault lies as much with the situation as with the people. Several years ago in Los Angeles, a passerby videotaped motorist Rodney King as he was being beaten by four police officers. The tape provoked outrage among the public, and a riot ensued when the officers were acquitted (a second, federal trial found them guilty). Although most people focused on the brutality of the four officers, it was also remarkable that many other policemen simply stood and watched them, making no effort to intervene or pull them away. After you finish this article, ask yourself what you would do if you and your friends saw someone being chased and beaten by someone on the street. Would you be able to resist the "diffusion of responsibility"?

In Groups, We Shrink From Loner's Heroics

The Los Angeles Times

March 22, 1991

The ghost of Kitty Genovese would sympathize with Rodney King. Genovese became the symbol of bystander apathy in America when, screaming for help, she was stabbed repeatedly and killed in front of her New York apartment building. Not one of the 38 neighbors who heard her, including those who came to their windows to watch, even called the police. People were horrified by this story, but it is repeated often. In fact, one of the things many people find appalling in the videotape of Rodney King's assault is the image of at least 11 police officers watching four of their colleagues administer the savage beating and doing nothing to intervene. Whatever is the matter with them, we wonder?

The answer from social science is: Nothing. It is normal for people in groups to think and act differently than they would on their own. Most people, if they observe some disaster or danger on their own—a woman being stabbed, a pedestrian slammed by a hit-and-run driver—will at least call for help. Many will even risk their own safety to intervene. But if they are in a group observing the same danger, they hold back. The reason is not necessarily that they are lazy, cowardly, or have other personality deficiencies; it has more to do with the nature of groups than with the nature of individuals.

In one experiment, for instance, students were seated in a room, either alone or in groups of three, as a staged emergency occurred: Smoke began pouring through the vents. Students who were on their own usually hesitated a minute, got up, checked the vents, and then went out to report what seemed like fire. But the students who were sitting in groups of three did not move. They sat there for six minutes, with smoke so thick they could barely see, rubbing their eyes and coughing.

In another experiment, psychologists staged a situation in which people overheard a crash, a scream, and a woman moaning that her ankle was broken. Fully 70 percent of those who were alone when the accident occurred went to her aid, compared to only 40 percent of those who heard her in the presence of another person.

For victims, obviously, there is no safety in numbers. Why? One reason is that if other people aren't doing anything, the individual assumes that nothing needs to be done. In the smoke-filled room study, the students in groups said they thought the smoke was caused by "steam pipes," "truth gas," or "leaks in the air conditioning"; not one said what the students on their own did: "I thought it was fire." In the lady-in-distress study, those who failed to help offered these reasons: "I thought she had a mild sprain"; "I didn't want to embarrass her."

Often, observers think nothing needs to be done because someone else has already taken care of it, and the more observers there are, the less

likely any one person is to call for help. In Albuquerque, N.M., 30 people watched for an hour and a half as a building burned to the ground before they realized that no one had called the fire department. Psychologists call this process "diffusion of responsibility" or "social loafing": The more people in a group, the lazier each individual in it becomes.

But there was no mistaking what those officers were doing to Rodney King. There was no way for those observers to discount the severity of the beating King was getting. What kept them silent?

One explanation, of course, is that they approved. They may have identified with the abusers, vicariously participating in a beating they rationalized as justified. The widespread racism in the LAPD and the unprovoked abuse of black people is undeniable. A friend of mine who runs a trucking company told me that one of her drivers, a 50-year-old black man, is routinely pulled over by Los Angeles cops for the flimsiest of reasons, "and made to lie down on the street like a dog." None of her white drivers has been treated this way.

Or the observers may have hated what was happening and been caught in the oldest of human dilemmas: do the moral thing, and be disliked, humiliated, embarrassed, and rejected. Our nation, for all its celebration of the Lone Ranger and the independent pioneer, does not really value the individual—at least, not when the person is behaving individually and standing up to the group. Countless studies have shown that people will go along rather than risk the embarrassment of being disobedient, rude, or disloyal.

And so the banality of evil is once again confirmed. Most people do not behave badly because they are inherently bad. They behave badly because they aren't paying attention, or they leave it to Harry, or they don't want to rock the boat, or they don't want to embarrass themselves or others if they're wrong.

Every time the news reports another story of a group that has behaved mindlessly, violently, and stupidly, including the inevitable members who are just going along, many people shake their heads in shock and anger at the failings of "human nature." But the findings of behavioral research can direct us instead to appreciate the conditions under which individuals in groups will behave morally or not.

Once we know the conditions, we can begin to prescribe antidotes. By understanding the impulse to diffuse responsibility, perhaps as individuals we will be more likely to act. By understanding the social pressures that reward groupthink, loyalty, and obedience, we can foster those that reward whistleblowing and moral courage. And, as a society, we can reinforce the belief that they also sin who only stand and watch.

24
THE SOURCES OF HAPPINESS

An enormous amount of psychological work has been devoted to the negative emotions—finding out why people become anxious, depressed, or angry. For the past few decades, however, many researchers have instead been studying why some people remain confident, cheerful, and calm even in the face of hardship and adversity. One clue to emotional well-being, the topic of the following book review, is the capacity for "flow," a state of involved absorption in what you are doing. Why do you suppose some people are able to experience this state routinely whereas others never do? How could work settings and classrooms be modified to maximize the opportunities for flow? How does flow differ from the usual definitions and meanings of "happiness"?

Review of *Flow: The Psychology of Optimal Experience*
By Mihaly Csikszentmihalyi
Harper & Row, 1990

The New York Times Book Review,
March 18, 1990

Years ago I came upon a melancholy fact: As the popularity of television increased in the 1950s and 1960s, the number of inventors and do-it-yourselfers declined precipitously. This sad phenomenon reflects the paradox of the pursuit of happiness. Given a choice, many people choose narcotic pleasures that dull the mind and quell its restless search for meaning. Yet in so doing, they give up the very activities that, in their complexity and challenge, offer the real promise of satisfaction.

For 20 years, psychologist Mihaly Csikszentmihalyi has been investigating the concept he calls *flow,* the state of involved enchantment that lies between boredom and anxiety. A person in flow is mentally involved in the challenge and intrinsic pleasure of the activity (and hence is not bored), yet lacks self-consciousness and performance apprehension (the hallmarks of anxiety). Flow takes energy and effort; it is not the same as fun, the teenager's grail, nor one of those moments of pure joy that seem to spring from nowhere. And it is not the same as the passive selflessness of "going with the flow." Usually, says Csikszentmihalyi, people experience flow while they are pursuing a goal, in the context of a set of rules. The goal may be a paramount ambition (building a better mousetrap), an interim ambition to improve a specific skill (walking a little farther on the exercise program today), or a temporary goal to keep from being bored to death (getting through a dull lecture by thinking of 436 uses for a brick).

Most people, Csikszentmihalyi argues, spend their lives alternating between work they dislike but feel obliged to do, and passive leisure activities that require no work but likewise offer no stimulation. "As a result," he says, "life passes in a sequence of boring and anxious experiences over which a person has little control." With flow, in contrast, "Alienation gives way to involvement, enjoyment replaces boredom, helplessness turns into a feeling of control, and psychic energy works to reinforce the sense of self, instead of being lost in the service of external goals."

As a theory of optimal experience, flow is a big improvement over Abraham Maslow's notion of self-actualization. Maslow regarded optimal experiences as frosting on the cake of life, possible only after one had met material needs for safety and security. Maslow's popular idea that basic needs must be met before people can pursue "higher order" needs for self-fulfillment has never been validated by research. On the contrary, many people who endure poverty, tragedy, and abuse nonetheless manage to find contentment and fulfillment.

The reason, Csikszentmihalyi argues, is not that misery builds character, but that the secret of contentment lies in controlling one's consciousness, and anybody can learn to do this. People describe having had flow experiences in every conceivable setting: climbing a mountain, working on an assembly line, living alone in the wilderness, enduring prolonged imprisonment. Flow doesn't require education, income, high intelligence, good health, or a spouse. It requires a mind: one that is willing to set challenges for itself and make the effort to meet them. In this respect, flow is another part of the cognitive revolution in psychology and psychotherapy: As scores of studies are finding, it is not so much what happens to people but how they interpret and explain what happens to them that determines their emotional well-being, their actions, their hopes, their ability to recover from adversity.

Csikszentmihalyi regards flow as the antidote to the twin evils of boredom and anxiety in all realms of experience, including education, work, sexuality, religion, and childrearing, and as a cure for social problems and psychological malaise. The lack of flow certainly does describe much of modern American life. But because he does not specify how society would have to change in order to get everyone flowing, he implies that the solution to our complex problems lies in millions of individuals learning to flow on their own. To expect such a miraculous cognitive transformation seems as dreamy, and unlikely, as counting on a mass religious conversion.

The author's enthusiasm for flow occasionally carries him away. Some of his examples of people who live their whole lives in a state of flow— never a passive moment! Never a mindless conversation! Never a dull activity that cannot be improved with active mental exercises!—made me self-consciously anxious and in need of my own escapist solution, a nap.

But as an analysis of individual psychology, flow is important, for it illuminates the psychological accuracy of what philosophers have been saying for centuries: that the way to happiness lies not in mindless hedonism but in mindful challenge, not in having unlimited opportunities but in focused possibilities, not in self-absorption but in absorption in the world, not in having it done for you but in doing it yourself.

25
THE MEANINGS OF SELF-ESTEEM

Everyone is in favor of self-esteem, but what is self-esteem, exactly? Feeling good about yourself? Feeling competent after you have accomplished something difficult? How would you separate self-esteem from narcissism, vanity, and pride? Where does self-esteem come from—pep talks? Mastering a new skill? Being told you're good, no matter how well you actually perform? This essay asks readers to define their terms, and it questions the common assumption that self-esteem leads straight to academic success and can be taught directly in the classroom. It also introduces the notion of "possible selves" that predict achievement better than a person's apparent self-regard does. If you were a teacher, how would you use psychological principles to promote genuine self-respect in your students? How high is your own self-esteem, and what "possible selves" do you envision for yourself?

Who Stole Grit From Self-Esteem?

The Los Angeles Times

September 16, 1991

I'm in favor of self-esteem. It's a good thing to have, if we judge from the depressed, defensive, or hostile behavior of people who don't have enough of it. I'm also in favor of educational and parental efforts designed to increase children's appreciation for their gender, ethnicity, or heritage.

Today, however, self-esteem is a mere shadow of its former self. Once, it referred to a fundamental sense of self-worth; today that meaning has narrowed into merely feeling good about oneself. Self-esteem used to rest on the daily acts of effort, care, and accomplishment that are the bedrock of character; now it rests on air, on *being* instead of *doing*. Healthy self-esteem used to fall between the equally unhealthy states of insecurity and narcissism; now it runs from "low" to "high," with no recognition that some people might feel too good about themselves, for no good reason.

None of this would matter, except that the murky psychological concept of self-esteem has become a blueprint for educational reform. Increasingly around the country, the new goal is to make children feel better about their gender or ethnicity.

In Detroit, a black teacher described the benefits of Afrocentric education for black boys. When they see a traffic light, he said, they should know it was invented by a black man, Garrett Morgan. Well, yes, they should. But what if the traffic light had been invented by a Chinese-

Lithuanian immigrant woman? Does that mean that black boys cannot aspire to become inventors or traffic engineers? Education historian Diane Ravitch once described an interview she read with a talented black runner who models herself after the ballet dancer Mikhail Baryshnikov. Baryshnikov, needless to say, is not black, female, a runner, or American-born, but he inspired this athlete because of his training and skill.

All students in American society, regardless of race, should learn about slavery, the civil-rights movement, and the contributions of black men and women. And each student would do well to study the specific, truthful history of his or her own culture—its venal, stupid, and murderous contributions to the world drama as well as its noble, smart, and generous ones. But as Ravitch points out, "Knowing about the travails and triumphs of one's forebears does not necessarily translate into either self-esteem or personal accomplishment."

In fact, self-esteem is not necessarily related to academic success. Delinquent teenage boys have very high self-esteem; they feel they are heroes to their peers. Black adolescent girls have higher self-esteem and confidence than white girls, but, to preserve this esteem in a system they perceive is always putting them down, they are also more likely to drop out of school and reject white authorities. White adolescent girls show a drop in self-esteem between childhood and high school, but many nonetheless go on to college.

Psychologist Hazel Marcus argues that a more revealing sign of adolescents' self-worth lies not in how good they feel about themselves, but in what they can envision for themselves in the future. People are guided by these "possible selves" that help us imagine what we can become (for better and worse) and that motivate us to reach our ideals. Possible selves are unrelated to self-esteem, but they are better predictors of behavior. Delinquent boys may have high self-esteem, but when asked to imagine their futures, most see themselves as being depressed, alone, addicted, or in jail.

So I propose a moratorium on self-esteem as a psychological concept and as an educational blueprint. Parents and educators would do better to focus on helping children achieve competence, perseverance, and optimism, which are the real contents of self-worth. They would do better to help children discover or invent their own best possible selves, to expand their visions of what they can become, even if no one of their gender, ethnicity, or culture has ever done it before. True self-esteem will follow.

26

SEXUAL ORIENTATION

Just as people often dichotomize gender, so they do with sexual orientation. But many social scientists have pointed out that "heterosexual" and "homosexual" behavior has varied historically and cross-culturally, and that even the view of the two categories as opposites is a relatively recent development that does not reflect a fact of nature. As you read this book review, ask yourself: Why do heterosexuals tend to view gay people, but not straight people, solely in terms of their sexuality? Why do so many people, gay and straight, think there must be a single cause of sexual orientation and behavior rather than many influences, including biological, learning, and situational ones? Do your feelings and possible prejudices about homosexuality or heterosexuality affect your beliefs about the origins of sexual orientation?

Review of *The Invention of Heterosexuality*
By Jonathan Ned Katz
Dutton, 1995

The New York Times Book Review,
April 16, 1995

If you are heterosexual, you will probably be inspired to make a joke or two about the title of this book. "Well, it's about time someone invented it," you'll want to say, or, "So that's what I've been doing all my life." Go ahead; Jonathan Ned Katz won't mind. He's got a swell sense of humor, and he appreciates the irony that a gay historian (his previous book was *Gay American History*) would be tackling the history of heterosexuality.

Heterosexuality, according to Katz, was invented in the 1860s in Germany. He is not, of course, talking about the invention of sexual feelings or acts between women and men, which presumably occurred a few times before 1860. He is talking about the invention of the *categories* "heterosexual" and "homosexual" and the idea that sexual behaviors clump into two opposite types. Katz shows how heterosexuality, as an idea and as an ideal, has changed over time, signifying "one particular historical arrangement of the sexes and their pleasures."

"Heterosexuality," he says, made its American debut in a medical journal in 1892, where it referred not to desire for the other sex but to desire for both sexes. It was considered a perversion, one of several "abnormal manifestations of the sexual appetite." The association of heterosexuality with perversion continued for several decades; as late as 1923, Merriam-Webster's dictionary called it a "morbid sexual passion for one of the opposite sex." But by 1934 it had become "a manifestation of sexual passion for one of the opposite sex; normal sexuality." (Note the term "opposite" sex, itself a relatively new way of regarding men and women.)

Katz traces the evolution of heterosexuality from its origins as a perverted desire to its present incarnation as normal sexuality. As the medical establishment claimed hegemony over sexual matters at the end of the nineteenth century, influenced by Freud, it transformed the discussion about sex from what was "natural" and "moral" to what was "normal" and "healthy." (At first this seemed like progress.) That done, physicians and psychiatrists sought to explain, and cure, those who were "abnormal" and "unhealthy." In the first decades of the twentieth century, Katz shows in his chapter "The heterosexual comes out," the mass media seized on and validated the concept of "the" heterosexual.

Scholars who study the origins of sexual orientation, like those who study differences between women and men, generally fall into two kinds: Those who think there are two kinds of people in the world, and those who don't. Are men and women opposite sexes? Are homosexuality and heterosexuality opposite orientations? The essentialist school holds that there is something fundamental, unchanging, and biologically wired in women and men, gay people and straight people, that causes their differences. The constructionist school holds that differences are largely due to economics, power inequities, and cultural forces, and that theories of difference have powerful social consequences. To illustrate this argument, constructionists like Katz have begun to examine the categories we consider normal instead of forever focusing on those who are different (women, blacks, Jews, and so forth). "By making the sex-normal the object of historical study," observes Katz, "we upset basic preconceptions." And so he does.

For readers unversed in social constructionism, this lively and provocative book will be a good introduction, especially to the ideas of Michel Foucault, whose monumental *History of Sexuality* challenged essentialist assumptions about sex. Unfortunately, Foucault also gave academics a new language, and from time to time Katz's prose runs aground in befogged Foucaultian swamps: "Heterosexuality, I now think, is invented in discourse as that which is outside discourse. It's manufactured in a particular discourse as that which is universal." In spite of these lapses and various arguments that readers may disagree with, Katz's overall message is important. It is not accidental that theories of difference flourish precisely when the differences in question are fading. Just when studies find that men and women are far more alike than different in abilities, nurturance, nastiness, wisdom, and foolishness, we get theories and television shows about how different our brains, psyches, and archetypes are. If the "gender gap" is narrowing, he argues, so is the "sexual orientation gap": even as the media emphasize biological differences between homosexuals and heterosexuals, the evidence shows a convergence in lifestyles, sexual practices, consumer values, diverse family arrangements, and endorsement of an ethic of sexual pleasure.

This convergence, of course, is precisely what is causing such anger from the right wing, which is determined to reinforce the alleged naturalness and superiority not only of heterosexuality but also of masculinity. And that is Katz's point: the terms heterosexuality and homosexuality do not simply describe variations in sexual behavior, but suggest that one way is right, healthy, and superior. "If homosexuals were to win society-wide equality with heterosexuals, there'd be no reason to distinguish them," Katz concludes. "The homosexual/heterosexual distinction would be retired from use, just as it was once invented."

Perhaps not. People in every culture and era have noticed variations in sexual orientation, whether they had labels for them or not. Moreover, such variations are pretty interesting, and I see no need to retire useful terms that describe them. Nor do I think it is necessary to perpetuate the dichotomy between biological contributions to behavior and social and cultural ones, as long as we heed the social constructionists' warnings against biological reductionism.

What we can and must dispense with are the value judgments that difference means deficiency and that numbers confer health or superiority. Left-handed people were once stigmatized, seen as abnormal, and subjected to all manner of supposed cures by right-handers convinced of their natural superiority. Today we regard left-handedness as a normal variation; it's no big deal. There is no reason we can't one day have the same attitude toward the extraordinary variation in human homosexualities . . . and heterosexualities.

PART V

MENTAL DISORDER
AND
TREATMENT

27

MEDICATING THE MIND

The increasing use of medication to treat not only severe mental and emotion-al problems but also more mundane ones raises many concerns about the drugs' possible long-term risks, the consequences for society, and the implica-tions for our notions of human nature and personality. Underlying these con-cerns is what we call the Jurassic Park Question: Just because we can do something (recreate dinosaurs from bits of DNA or, in this case, use medication to treat any emotional problem or "cure" personality flaws), does that mean we should do it? When is drug therapy warranted and helpful, and when does it become "cosmetic pharmacology"?

Review of *Listening to Prozac: A Psychiatrist Explores Antidepressant Drugs and the Remaking of the Self*
By Peter Kramer
Viking, 1993

The Los Angeles Times Book Review,
June 13, 1993

A decade ago, two books fore-told the current state of psy-chiatry. In *Mind, Mood, and Medicine*, Paul Wender and Donald Klein celebrated the "new biopsychi-atry." Mental illness, they said, once thought to result from poorly func-tioning defense mechanisms, is now known to result from poorly function-ing brain mechanisms. Thanks to the success of drugs where the "talking cure" has failed, they predicted, peo-ple will no longer suffer from depres-sion, anxiety, anger, or even the blues. The right drug can be tailor-made to fix those deficient neurotransmitters.

At the same time, with much less fanfare, Jonas Robitscher published *The Powers of Psychiatry*, in which he warned of the potential dangers of medicalizing normal emotional prob-lems. Because drugs are easy to administer, he predicted, too many psychiatrists will prescribe them indiscriminately, without asking what a person might be depressed, anxious, or fearful about. Robitscher's quiet cautions were generally drowned out in the subsequent decade by the noisy enthusiasm of biopsychiatrists, and by the economic juggernaut of drug and insurance companies that were promoting drugs for mood disorders.

Peter Kramer, like many of his fellow psychiatrists, has discovered the wonders of pharmacology, partic-

95

ularly the antidepressant Prozac (fluoxetine). Established antidepressants are considered "dirty" drugs because they affect many bodily systems and thus have unpredictable results and side effects. Prozac was heralded as a "clean" drug, a high-tech concoction designed to target a single neurotransmitter in the brain (serotonin) and thus to have specific beneficial effects on depression. Watching his patients thrive on the drug made Kramer a convert—quite a convert, considering that his previous book was *Moments of Engagement: intimate psycho-therapy in a technological age.* "Spending time with patients who responded to Prozac had transformed my views about what makes people the way they are," Kramer writes. He called this phenomenon "listening to Prozac." "I had come to see inborn, biologically determined temperament where before I had seen slowly acquired, history-laden character." This book grew out of Kramer's curiosity about two puzzles: How can a medication dramatically alter a person's sense of self? What does the success of medication tell us about the origins and nature of mood, personality, and the self?

As a social scientist, I am familiar with the research on all kinds of therapy—biochemical, psychoanalytic, and psychological—but I am not a psychotherapist and have no vested interest in any one approach. I am not opposed to medication on principle; I know harrowing stories of people who spent fruitless years in talk therapy and then were saved by the right drug. But I also know harrowing stories of people who have been dangerously and mindlessly overmedicated for normal troubles. Both errors are common in the current turf war among mental-health professionals for the hearts, minds, and dollars of people with problems.

Kramer is a wonderful writer, and his readers will learn much about the new research on temperament and personality, biological theories of mood disorders, and the behind-the-scenes stories of how psychiatric drugs were discovered or invented. His chapters, laced with illuminating case studies, chronicle the seemingly miraculous effects of Prozac on compulsion, perfectionism, low self-esteem, stress and trauma, shyness, irritability, anxiety, panic, hypersensitivity to rejection, need for attention, lack of assertiveness and inability to take risks, inhibition of pleasure, sluggishness of thought, and *dysthymia,* a condition of chronic melancholy. While admitting that scientists really don't know much about the brain, depression, or drugs at the moment, Kramer endorses the biopsychiatric prediction that new drugs will one day "modify inborn predisposition" and "repair traumatic damage to personality." "As we have access to yet more specific drugs," he says, "our accuracy in targeting individual traits will improve."

But *Listening to Prozac* is most valuable for the provocative questions that Kramer asks throughout the book, particularly in the last chapter. Should he provide medication for reasons of "cosmetic psychopharmacology," not for debilitating mental illness but simply to help patients feel better, think sharper, and have a psychological advantage at work? He wonders whether we will end up with "Psychic steroids for mental gymnastics, medicinal attacks on the humors, antiwallflower compound—these might be hard to resist." He admits that the possibility of reaching into the personality to alter a single trait—to perk up low self-esteem, perhaps, or mental agility—"has worrisome implications, not only as regards the arrogance of doctors but as regards the subtly coercive power of convention." I'll say.

Kramer also recognizes the cultural context of emotional problems. Because a personality trait such as "perfectionism" might be normal and desirable in one society or relationship but a problem or liability in another, Kramer wonders which should be fixed—the person or the environment. "Should a person with a personality style that might succeed in a different social setting have to change her personality (by means of drugs!) in order to find fulfillment?" he asks. Many women, observes Kramer, do not have an "illness" of depression; they have a coping strategy that is not rewarded in contemporary society. Should women be given Prozac to help them succeed in an aggressive, combative, competitive system?

Moreover, Kramer recognizes that there might be tragic and unforeseen *social* consequences of thousands of otherwise rational *individual* decisions to improve one's personality through modern chemistry. Do we want a brave new world in which no one suffers from miserable moods or chronic complaints? "Much of the insight and creative achievement of the human race," Kramer allows, "is due to the discontent, guilt, and critical eye of dysthymics."

And yet, as soon as Kramer raises these challenging questions, he dances away from them. It's as if he is so excited by the liberating potential of medication and of the biological model of personality that he doesn't want to hear what his own cautionary side is telling him. So he thinks we can trust to a native suspicion about drugs to save us from overmedicating our personalities, even though he immediately adds that this "may be flimsy protection against the allure of medication. Do we feel secure in counting on our irrationality, our antiscientific prejudice, to save us from the ubiquitous cultural pressures for enhancement?" I sure don't. And neither do the drug companies. How many people will be "irrational" enough to resist yet another pill that promises slimness? How many people are going to make the effort to fix social institutions if they can take a pill to help them adjust to existing ones?

Kramer actually raises enough concerns about medication to have written another book called *Worrying About Prozac*. He correctly dismisses the hysteria that followed Prozac's early fame, the false alarms that Prozac was turning people into killers and suicides. But his book is full of cautions: the people for whom it doesn't work, who don't like losing their rough edges, who report feeling that Prozac numbs the "moral sensibility"; the unpleasant side effects, such as nausea, headache, and constant restlessness; the fact that "concern over unforeseen or tardive [late-appearing] effects" is realistic because we don't know the long-term effects of Prozac. This Kramer announces on the *last page* of the book.

This book is good as far as it goes, but I wish it went further. Readers won't learn anything, for example, about the successful treatments for mood disorders that require neither years of psychoanalysis nor medication. Kramer devotes a tiny paragraph to cognitive therapy, acknowledging only that it is "lately much in vogue"; you bet it is, because it works. Controlled studies find that cognitive therapy—a relatively brief program of treatment in which people learn how their own perceptions maintain their anxieties and griefs—is often just as effective as medication for most mood disorders, including panic attacks, without side effects and long-term risks. (Again, no single therapy works for everybody.)

I recommend *Listening to Prozac*, but for readers who know little about the relative merits of medication and different psychotherapies, I also recommend some balance: Seymour Fisher and Roger Greenberg's *The Limits of Biological Treatments for Psychological Distress*, Louise Armstrong's *And They Call It Help: The psychiatric policing of America's children*, or Elliot Valenstein's *Blaming the Brain: The real truth about drugs and mental health*. When you listen to Prozac or the many other popularly used drugs in these books, you will hear a very different message.

28

THE LIMITS OF MEDICATION

Six years after the publication of Listening to Prozac, *antidepressants had become even bigger business. They were being prescribed not only for depression, but also for anxiety disorders such as panic attacks and obsessive-compulsive behavior, and even for shyness and "social phobias." This essay, like the one preceding it, tries to avoid either-or thinking about medications by examining the benefits and risks of medication for emotional and personality problems—and by asking, "What information are the drug companies not giving us?" In assessing the value of any therapeutic intervention or medication, critical thinkers need to ask: What are its strengths, weaknesses, and risks? Is the person or company promoting this solution telling me the whole story? In the case of medication, might there be less risky solutions that are just as effective, which I could try first?*

We're Only Hearing About the Quick Fix

The Los Angeles Times

May 7, 1999

"**D**oes your life have signs of persistent anxiety?" the ad asks. "Should you see your doctor? . . . Ask your doctor about a nonhabit-forming medicine."

People constantly are being encouraged to see their doctors for help with their fears, phobias, and worries. I have a friend who has had a fear of cats all her life; another who has panic attacks if she drives on a freeway. If my friends went to a physician or psychiatrist, chances are that they would come away with a prescription for medication or possibly spend several years trying to find the origins of their fears. They would learn nothing at all about a proved nonmedical kind of psychotherapy that would be far more likely to help them.

The drug companies have succeeded brilliantly in persuading the public that antidepressants are the treatment of choice for feelings that range from the mild blues to severe depression. Now, they are launching a campaign to persuade everyone with feelings from mild anxiety to severe panic disorder to use them, too. SmithKline Beecham is awaiting clearance to market its antidepressant, Paxil, for "social phobias" and extreme shyness. Ads soon will tout Paxil as a solution for people who are "allergic to people."

And yet, dozens of studies have shown conclusively that the effectiveness of any antidepressant, including the much-heralded Prozac, is far more modest than consumers have been led to believe. The public is largely unaware of the contradictory and disconfirming evidence about antidepressants and, more important, of why they are unaware of it.

The massive economic power of the pharmaceutical industry now controls much of the basic research on mental disorders, sexual problems, and psychological functioning conducted in this country. Drug companies may embargo that research, deciding whether, when, and where it may be published, if at all. They set up their own research institutes, sponsor professional conferences and fund scientists. They can thereby direct the kinds of questions scientists investigate—and the kinds of answers they find. Sex researchers can get thousands of dollars from Pfizer, which manufactures Viagra, to study medical theories of sexual dysfunction, but not a cent for the study of kissing, coercion, or communication.

The influence of drug companies is sometimes buried under layers of corporate structure. In *Blaming the Brain*, neuropsychologist Elliot Valenstein offers the example of PCS Health Systems, an agency that provides information to physicians, pharmacies, and health care managers on ways to "improve patient care and lower health care costs." PCS informed its constituents that Prozac is the antidepressant of choice, being cheaper than Zoloft or Paxil and more effective. It did not report any of the considerable evidence disputing this claim. PCS Health Systems is owned by Eli Lilly, which manufactures Prozac.

But antidepressants have serious limitations. First, a large part of the effectiveness of any new drug for emotional problems is a result of the enthusiasm surrounding it and the expectation of a quick cure. When these "placebo effects" decline, many drugs turn out to be neither as effective as promised nor as widely applicable. Findings like this are well known to research psychologists. In their analysis of 19 studies involving more than 2,000 depressed patients, Irving Kirsch and Guy Saperstein found that 75 percent of the drugs' effectiveness was due entirely to the placebo effect or other nonchemical factors.

Second, little or no research has been done on the effects of taking antidepressants (or many other drugs) for many years. Already there are suspicions that antidepressants, including Prozac, may cause cardiovascular problems in some vulnerable people after long-term use. Most new drugs are often tested on only a few hundred people for only a few weeks, even then the drug is one that patients might take for many years. For example, the Food and Drug Administration warned that "Because clomipramine [for obsessive-compulsive disorder] has not been systematically evaluated for long-term use (more than 10 weeks), physicians should periodically reevaluate the long-term usefulness of the drug for individual patients." In an era of managed care, how many of them will do so?

Third, because antidepressants tend to have unpleasant side effects— including dry mouth, headaches, constipation, nausea, restlessness, gastrointestinal problems, weight gain, and, in many patients, decreased sexual desire and delayed orgasm—the large majority of people given these medications stop taking them. Such individuals are likely to relapse as soon as they do.

The alternative to medication is not some generic form of talk therapy. My friend with the cat phobia spent years with psychiatrists, and they all agreed that it was a traumatic nightmare in her childhood that first generated her fear. Unfortunately, insight about the origins of one's fears or blues does little or nothing to alleviate them.

However, a specific kind of psychotherapy repeatedly has been found to be beneficial for emotional and behavioral disorders such as depression, anger, anxiety, panic attacks, stress-related illnesses, and obsessive-compulsive disorder: cognitive-behavior therapy, a program that helps people identify and change the thoughts and actions that are keeping them unhappy or fearful. In hundreds of studies involving thousands of people, cognitive-behavior therapy has been shown either to be more effective than medication or as effective, without side effects and high relapse rates.

Obviously, some people benefit from medication. It would be as foolish to claim that cognitive-behavior therapy helps everyone as it is to claim that drugs do. And, unfortunately, many therapists are uninformed about the benefits of cognitive and behavioral procedures and unskilled in their application. A person suffering from panic disorder would do better to take an antidepressant than spend months or years with a psychotherapist who is ignorant of these procedures.

But in this biomedical age, consumers must protect themselves against the one-sided story they will hear from drug companies, ads, and physicians. We must ask about side effects, long-term risks, and alternative therapies that might be just as effective. We must be alert to any financial interests that researchers may have in a product or finding. And we must try to resist the allure of the next miracle cure for the next everyday problem. If hope could be bottled, its sales would leave those of Viagra in the dust.

29
THE POLITICS OF DIAGNOSIS: "PMS" AND THE DSM

This essay tells the story of how the symptoms associated with menstruation became packaged into a full-blown psychiatric diagnosis. It tells a more general story as well: about the enormous growth in psychiatric "disorders" in recent decades, as problems that were once considered a normal part of life have become pathologized and medicalized. What do these developments tell us about the effects of cultural beliefs and economic interests on concepts of normality and abnormality? What do you suppose would happen if "hypertestosterone aggression disorder" were proposed as an official mental illness? Why is more attention paid to women's hormones and moods than to men's?

You Haven't Come Very Far, Baby

The Los Angeles Times

March 4, 1993

In spite of protests from dozens of women psychiatrists and psychologists, the American Psychiatric Association has, in its wisdom, decided that "premenstrual syndrome" is a certifiable mental disorder. They won't call it PMS, of course. Their version has a fancier name: "Premenstrual Dysphoric Disorder." By any name, it isn't just a cute label for some women's premenstrual discomfort or a funny subject for tampon ads and sitcoms. It's big business, and its pernicious effects are apparent in the story of how it became a mental illness.

The *Diagnostic and Statistical Manual of Mental Disorders*, the bible of psychiatry, contains a list of mental disorders that are compensable by insurance companies. As the territory of psychiatry and clinical psychology has expanded, so has the number of treatable problems. In 1968, the manual contained 66 disorders; in the 1987 edition, it had 261 disorders. *[Note: and by the fourth edition in 1994, it had nearly 400 disorders.]* The DSM includes not only serious disorders such as schizophrenia and other psychoses, but also normal problems for which people seek help, including tobacco dependence, reading problems, and sexual complaints.

Now, there's nothing wrong with that, as long as we understand that most definitions of mental disorder are a matter of subjective clinical consensus, not science. As attitudes changed, psychiatrists voted out many biased old "disorders" such as childhood masturbation disorder, nymphomania, and homosexuality. And they

102

have voted in disorders that reflect modern biases, such as "inhibited sexual desire" and, now, "Premenstrual Dysphoric Disorder," or PMDD for short. Many scientists are appalled at this decision, arguing that the scholarly evidence for the diagnosis is lousy and the social implications for women are dangerous.

Psychiatrists get very huffy about anyone who suggests that PMDD is just PMS in fancy dress. PMDD, they say, is meant to describe only the tiny percentage of women who have severe physical and emotional symptoms associated with menstruation. But if that is so, why should a problem with menstruation be included in a manual of *mental disorders*? Thyroid abnormalities and other physical problems cause mood and behavior changes too, but we don't regard these changes as a psychiatric illness. There is no diagnosis, say, for "chronic back pain depressive disorder."

The list of criteria for diagnosing PMDD gives the game away. A woman must have five of these symptoms: mood swings; anger or irritability; anxiety or tension; depressed mood or self-deprecating thoughts; decreased interest in usual activities; fatigue; change in appetite; sleeplessness or sleepiness; physical symptoms such as breast tenderness or swelling, headaches, muscle pain, "bloating," and weight gain (those latter physical symptoms are all normal aspects of menstruation, of course). How does this list differ from the popular concept of PMS? Not at all. What is to prevent psychiatrists from overdiagnosing this "disorder," as they already

do? Where is the stipulation that this diagnosis must depend on measuring a woman's hormone levels, to separate a woman with PMDD from one whose problem is depression?

Moreover, the idea that these symptoms constitute a disorder at all overlooks these research findings:

• When men keep daily diaries of their moods and physical symptoms (such as headaches, insomnia, muscle pain, fatigue, and irritability), their symptoms do not differ, on the average, from women's. Actually, men are somewhat more irritable all through the month than women are. Why then are women's mood changes a disorder, while men's are normal ups and downs?

• In spite of 50 years of efforts to find negative effects of menstruation, research consistently shows that the menstrual cycle has no effect on mental abilities, work, or academic tests. In contrast, high testosterone is associated with violence, drug abuse, and impulsive behavior. Yet psychiatrists have not felt it necessary to invent "hypertestosterone aggression disorder."

• Whatever PMS or PMDD are, there is no treatment for them. Controlled studies find that progesterone, most commonly prescribed, is no more effective than a placebo. But "cures" are a thriving business. The diagnosis is quick, easy, and compensable. Doctors and drug companies will make money off it.

Many women embrace the language of PMS because they feel it

validates the normal changes of the menstrual cycle and, let's be candid, because it gives them an excuse to blow off steam at least once a month. (The comparable excuse for men is drinking.) But women pay a big price for buying PMS. Imagine the fun the press would have with a female candidate for office who had been treated for "premenstrual dysphoric disorder." And as a student of mine once said, "I like being able to use PMS as an excuse for losing my temper, but I hate it when I'm mad at my boyfriend and he won't listen to me, saying, 'Oh, you just must have PMS.'" Precisely.

Women are already reporting that their legitimate complaints in the workplace and the home are being ridiculed as evidence of "PMS." In bestowing its self-serving approval to this label, the psychiatric establishment feeds the prejudice that women's hormones, but not men's, are a cause of mental illness. That's just ancient superstition in pompous new jargon.

[NOTE: The fourth edition (1994) of the Diagnostic and Statistical Manual of Mental Disorders still includes PMDD, in spite of extensive disagreement among its own task force members. The fourth edition also includes, among many other new disorders, "caffeine intoxication disorder," "caffeine-induced sleep disorder," "mathematics disorder," and "disorder of written expression."]

30

THINKING CRITICALLY
ABOUT PSYCHOTHERAPY

The book reviewed in this essay raises important questions about the state of psychotherapeutic training and practice. When you are finished reading, ask yourself: Do psychotherapists have too much influence in our society, and if so, how did that come to pass? What are the reasons for the growing gap between psychological scientists and psychotherapists? Many practitioners believe that psychological research is largely irrelevant to the work they do with clients; do you agree, or do you think they should keep informed about new research? How can a consumer tell a capable therapist from one who uses inappropriate, unvalidated, or even harmful methods, or who is uninformed about such important findings in psychological science as which treatments are best for which problems?

Review of *House of Cards:*
Psychology and Psychotherapy Built on Myth
By Robyn M. Dawes
Free Press, 1994

The Los Angeles Times Book Review,
May 8, 1994

I no longer tell people I'm a "social psychologist"; they think it means I'm a therapist who likes parties. They listen politely as I try to explain that *research* psychologists—the people who conduct empirical studies of child development, thinking, memory, prejudice, mob violence, language, or any other aspect of human behavior— are not the same as *clinical* psychologists or any other kind of psychotherapist. My efforts usually fall on deaf ears. "How many patients do you see a week?" they ask, or maybe, "What do you make of this really interesting dream I had?"

It was not always thus. In 1959 the American Psychological Association (APA) had 18,000 members, of whom only 2,500 specialized in clinical or counseling work. By 1988, there were 68,000 members, of whom 40,000 were clinicians or counselors. Today the proportion of the APA's membership accounted for by these two groups is even greater, and in addition there are many therapists who are not Ph.D. psychologists but who have various other degrees (such as marriage and family counselors or social workers) or no degrees at all. Accordingly, the word "psychologist" has, in the public mind, become synonymous with "therapist."

The reason this matters, argues Robyn Dawes in *House of Cards*, is the widening gap between researchers and therapists in *what they know* and *how they know* it. In the rapid and explosive growth in the sheer numbers of therapists, the practice of psychology has abandoned its original commitment to establish a mental health profession based on research findings, using well-validated techniques and principles. On the contrary, Dawes shows, the training of most psychotherapists has come loose from its original moorings in scientific procedures (such as the use of control groups before concluding that one method is better than another) and empirically based knowledge (such as observing how children actually recover from trauma, instead of assuming that they never do without therapy). Instead, many therapists actively disdain research as being irrelevant to their practices; they know, they say, from "clinical experience" and "intuition" what is right.

Such claims make Dawes angry, as over and over again he reveals the unwarranted arrogance of therapists who make such claims. Drawing on more than 300 empirical investigations, he shows why "professionals' claims to superior intuitive insight, understanding, and skill as therapists are simply invalid." Psychotherapy has grown and achieved status, Dawes observes, while ignoring research that contradicts its claims, adopting principles that are "known to be untrue," and using techniques "known to be invalid." Dawes debunks dozens of incorrect ideas promulgated by psychotherapists who apparently know little or nothing of psychological research. For example:

• *Belief:* Abused children invariably become abusers; children of alcoholics become alcoholic. *Fact:* The majority do not.
• *Belief:* Memory works like a tape recorder, faithfully recording everything that happens from the moment of birth. *Fact:* For normal physiological and psychological reasons, adults do not remember events that happened roughly before the age of three years. A memory is not recorded in perfect form. It is reconstructed from aspects of the event, subsequent interpretations, and one's current feelings and beliefs about the past event, and it may be revised over time, and feelings and beliefs change.
• *Belief:* Self-esteem is the key ingredient in well-being and achievement; low self-esteem is the main cause of drug abuse, violence, and teenage pregnancy. *Fact:* Literally thousands of studies have failed to support this belief. The California Task Force on Self-Esteem, Dawes observes, performed an unintended public service: It demonstrated that "the Holy Grail of pop psychology"— the belief that high self-esteem is the ticket to happiness and low self-esteem is the cause of social problems—"is nothing more than a mirage."